DEREGULATION AND GLOBALIZATION

The American Enterprise Institute Trade in Services Series

COMPETING IN A CHANGING WORLD ECONOMY PROJECT

Deregulation and Globalization: Liberalizing International Trade in Air Services — *Daniel M. Kasper*

Global Competition in Financial Services: Market Structure, Protection, and Trade Liberalization — *Ingo Walter*

International Trade in Business Services: Accounting, Advertising, Law, and Management Consulting — *Thierry J. Noyelle and Anna B. Dutka*

International Trade in Construction, Design, and Engineering Services — *James R. Lee and David Walters*

International Trade in Films and Television Programs — *Steven S. Wildman and Stephen E. Siwek*

International Trade in Ocean Shipping Services: The United States and the World — *Lawrence J. White*

When Countries Talk: International Trade in Telecommunications Services — *Jonathan David Aronson and Peter F. Cowhey*

International Trade in Services: An Overview and Blueprint for Negotiations — *Geza Feketekuty*

Deregulation and Globalization

Liberalizing International Trade in Air Services

Daniel M. Kasper

An American Enterprise Institute/Ballinger Publication

Ballinger Publishing Company, Cambridge, Massachusetts
A Subsidiary of Harper & Row, Publishers, Inc.

International Standard Book Number: 0-88730-233-5

Library of Congress Catalog Card Number: 88-11967

Printed in the United States of America.

Library of Congress Cataloging-in-Publication Data

Kasper, Daniel M.
Deregulation and globalization: liberalizing international trade in air services / Daniel M. Kasper.
p. cm. — (The American Enterprise Institute series on trade in services)
Includes index.
ISBN 0-88730-233-5
1. Airlines—United States—Deregulation. 2. Airlines—Deregulation. I. Title.
II. Series: American Enterprise Institute series on trade in services.
HE9803.A35K37 1988
387.7'1—dc19 88-11967
CIP

CONTENTS

LIST OF FIGURES

LIST OF TABLES

EDITOR'S FOREWORD

The American Enterprise Institute's *Trade in Services Series* represents an important step toward creating the policy alternatives necessary to enhance the international competitiveness of American services.

The series is part of a larger, continuing AEI project, *Competing in a Changing World Economy*. Launched in 1983, this project has produced a wealth of publications, seminars, and conferences, analyzing the most significant policy challenges confronting U.S. policymakers in the areas of international trade and finance, science and technology policy, and human capital development.

Early in the project, we concluded that the United States would be successful in its drive to initiate a new round of trade negotiations with the other major trading nations, under the auspices of the General Agreement on Tariffs and Trade (GATT). We also chose to concentrate our resources on the new issues that would be placed on the table in that round: trade in services, intellectual property, and trade-related investment. In September 1986, at Punta del Este, Uruguay, the United States and the other members of GATT did indeed reach an agreement to launch a new multilateral round of trade negotiations, the Uruguay Round. Trade in services, along with intellectual property and investment issues, was included on the agenda. Hence, over the next several years negotiators in Geneva and top policy officials in all the major trading nations will face the formidable task of forging trading rules for these new issues.

In the area of services, a number of countries, including the United States, have produced individual, national studies of service trade liberalization. Yet government and private-sector officials agree that these studies are only a first step, and that substantial research remains to be done in key service sectors before major policy questions can be answered regarding a new service trade regime.

Designed to fill this policy gap, *Trade in Services* brings together eleven outstanding writers who have committed their expertise to analyzing the seven key service sector industries:

- Aviation—Daniel M. Kasper, Harbridge House
- Banking—Ingo Walter, Graduate School of Business Administration, New York University
- Construction—James R. Lee, American University, and David Walters, Staff Economist, Office of the U.S. Trade Representative
- Professional services—Thierry J. Noyelle and Anna B. Dutka, Conservation of Human Resources, Columbia University
- Shipping—Lawrence J. White, Member, Federal Home Loan Bank Board, on leave from the Graduate School of Business Administration, New York University
- Telecommunications: Information and Data Processing—Jonathan David Aronson, School of International Relations, University of Southern California, and Peter F. Cowhey, Department of Political Science, University of California at San Diego
- Telecommunications: Motion Pictures, Television, and Prerecorded Entertainment—Steven S. Wildman and Stephen E. Siwek, Economists Incorporated

In addition, Geza Feketekuty, of the Office of the U.S. Trade Representative, has written an overview volume for the series.

All of the books in the series embody two main goals: first, to analyze the dynamics of international competition for each of the seven industries, identifying existing and potential barriers to trade; and second, to formulate and assess policy approaches for opening service markets through an umbrella service agreement and subsequent individual sector agreements in GATT.

A related goal is to disseminate the results of our research through conferences and seminars, televised forums, and a variety of publication formats. We aim to make our findings known to government officials, trade experts, the business and financial communities, and concerned members of the public. To that end, during 1987 we convened major conferences in London, Geneva, and Washington, and in early 1988 the team of authors traveled to Tokyo and Singapore. Thus, as with all AEI projects, we have sought to ensure that the studies not only make a significant contribution to scholarship but also become an important factor in the decision making and negotiating processes.

In addition to the authors, who have produced outstanding books, we would like to thank John H. Jackson, Hessel E. Yntema Professor of Law at the University of Michigan, and Gardner Patterson, who for many years served in the GATT Secretariat. Both of these men provided invaluable help and guidance as advisers to the project.

—Claude E. Barfield
Coordinator
Competing in a Changing World Economy

PREFACE

The air services sector offers interesting and valuable lessons for those seeking to liberalize trade in services. At a time of increasing interest in bilateral trade agreements, the airline industry provides a laboratory for evaluating the results of more than forty years of trade under a regime of bilateral agreements. Since the United States has pursued a bilateral liberalization strategy for the past decade, air services also offer an opportunity to evaluate the efficacy of bilateral trade agreements as vehicles for liberalizing trade in services.

Drawing upon a long standing academic interest in international trade and the GATT, an intimate knowledge of the airline industry, and several years as an international aviation policymaker and negotiator for the U.S. government, I argue that the economic forces set loose by U.S. deregulation are restructuring the world's airline industry in ways that cannot be readily accommodated within the existing bilateral regime. Moreover, neither a bilateral system nor a GATT-based multilateral regime is adequate to deal with the twin problems of expanding market access and ensuring that competition is not distorted by hidden barriers and unfair trade practices.

To achieve true liberalization in air services, a new approach will be required, one that focuses on securing agreement among a relatively small group of liberal trading partners willing to abide by a strict condition designed to ensure open and vigorous competition on a reasonably level playing field. Such an approach, I argue, will preclude the use of unconditional most-favored-nation and national treatment, two principles fundamental to the existing GATT legal regime for trade in goods.

For those readers with only selective areas of interest in the air services industry, I offer the following roadmap to the book. Chapter 1 provides background information and an overview that are important prerequisites for the analyses developed in the subsequent chapters. I recommend it for all readers. Those who are not experts in international aviation will find Chapter 2 helpful in understanding the structure and economics of the industry, while Chapter 3 describes the international legal regime governing international air services. Chapter 4 identifies the principal barriers to liberalization in this sector and is recommended for all readers. Chapter 5 analyzes U.S. efforts to extend deregulation to international airline markets and should be of particular interest to trade negotiators and policymakers. It is also recommended for political scientists and others with an interest in the interaction of domestic and international interest groups in the development and implementation of U.S. economic policy. The final chapters identify important negotiating and trade policy implications both for air services and broader trade talks. Chapter 6 analyzes the applicability of key GATT principles to air services and highlights some shortcomings of the GATT that have important implications for trade policy in other sectors, while Chapter 7 evaluates alternative negotiating strategies. Both are recommended for all readers.

I would like to give special thanks to Claude Barfield of the Competing in a Changing World Economy Project at the American Enterprise Institute. I am also grateful to my colleagues at Harbridge House for their support throughout the book's long gestation period.

Parts and earlier versions of this work have appeared elsewhere. I am grateful to the following organizations for giving me the opportunity to refine my thinking on their pages: "Liberalizing Trade in Air Services: How We Get There from Here," *The World Economy*, March 1988; "Toward Open Skies Worldwide," *The Wall Street Journal*, 3 August 1987; "Liberalizing Trans-Atlantic Air Services," *Europe Magazine*, December

1987; and "Freeing Trade in the Skies," *The Journal of Commerce*, February 2, 1988.

A number of people have offered helpful comments and advice in the development of this work. These include Jonathan Aronson, Peter Cowhey, Hugh Corbet, Geza Feketekuty, Brian Hindley, John Jackson, Daniel Kaplan, Michael Levine, Geoffrey Lipman, Jeffrey Shane, and Judith Connor Trent. Without the secretarial assistance of Sandi Russell, Clare O'Loughlin, and Julie Lee, the manuscript could never have been completed.

Finally, to Sherry for her patience and support, to Brendan and Jeremy for permitting me to monopolize the computer, and to my parents—only some of whose skills in writing and editing have been inherited by their children—my special thanks and gratitude.

DEREGULATION AND GLOBALIZATION

1
INTRODUCTION

By the year 2000, and perhaps sooner, most of the free world's air services are likely to be provided by a score of large multinational airlines competing on a global scale. For an industry that, until quite recently, could be accurately described as a series of local monopolies connected by a set of equally protected international routes, the change will be little short of revolutionary. Nonetheless, careful analysis will show that the emergence of a global airline industry by the turn of the century is neither farfetched nor unrealistic but rather the natural and, I believe, predictable result of fundamental economic and political forces now at work in the world economy.

The reason for the change is clear. Airline deregulation in the United States has led to sharp increases in competition and major structural changes in the U.S. airline industry. In turn, the powerful economic forces unleashed by U.S. domestic deregulation and its companion, the competitive international aviation policy, have forced foreign airlines and governments alike to accept more market liberalization than most would have chosen voluntarily.

The external effects of deregulation are most visible today in Europe and in the Pacific Basin. Since the United States deregulated air services in 1978, Canada, New Zealand, Australia, the United Kingdom, Japan, and the People's Republic of China, among others, have substantially deregulated their domestic air service markets and most are actively considering privatization of—or have actually privatized—state-owned airlines.

Plagued by small domestic markets, by restrictive international agreements, and often by inefficient airlines, nations in these regions have begun to support increased liberalization not necessarily because they believe in its virtues, but because they view liberalization as essential to the viability of their airlines in an increasingly competitive marketplace.[1] Scandinavia is an interesting case in point. After almost a decade of vigorous resistance to U.S. efforts to liberalize the existing air services agreement, Norway, Sweden, Denmark, and their flag airline, SAS, reversed position and proposed a liberal, "open skies" agreement to an incredulous U.S. delegation. The explanation for the change of heart is easy to find: liberalization is the best means of assuring access for SAS to the huge U.S. and internal European Community markets that are critical to the airline's long-term viability.

PARADIGMS AND REALITY: AN OVERVIEW OF INTERNATIONAL AIR SERVICES

A genuinely liberal regime for air services would permit firms to enter and exit markets without government restrictions; to select which markets they would serve; to tailor their products, services, and capacity to meet perceived market demands; and to set prices independently and competitively in a marketplace free of distortions caused by government subsidies, protectionism, and other measures favoring local airlines over their foreign competitors. Such a regime does not exist in international aviation today.

Until 1978, when the United States adopted its competitive aviation policy, international air services were routinely subjected to strict limits on entry, routing, and capacity. Prices charged for international air services were also subject to government control,[2] but governments had largely ceded that control to airlines under the auspices of the International Air Transport Association (IATA). Despite significant liberalization over the past decade, however, substantial barriers continue to impair both trade and transborder investment in air services.

The current barriers to liberalized trade in air services can be usefully grouped into four categories: (1) bilateral restrictions that prevent entry or directly restrict the competitiveness of foreign airlines; (2) domestic regulatory systems; (3) restrictions in ancillary domestic markets that impair a foreign carrier's ability to compete; and (4) subsidization and state ownership of airlines.

Bilateral Restrictions

Without the consent of a sovereign state, an airline lacks the right to carry traffic to or from that nation's territory. Airlines typically obtain such rights through bilateral agreements negotiated between national governments whose airlines wish to provide such services. These agreements govern entry, capacity, traffic, fares, and routes and are often the most formidable barriers to liberalized trade in air services. The extension of the sovereignty concept to traffic originating or arriving within national boundaries encourages countries to trade access to each other's traffic. Under these circumstances, countries that generate a large volume of traffic (the "haves") are strongly motivated to protect "their" traffic from the "have nots" in order to preserve it for trading to other "haves" in exchange for access to their larger traffic pools.

Domestic Regulatory Policies

With the right neither to enter foreign domestic markets nor to establish an airline in a foreign jurisdiction, otherwise efficient airlines may be prevented from attaining the economies of scale and scope necessary to compete successfully in world air services markets. Thus, regulatory policies that exclude foreign airlines from domestic markets or restrict their ability to compete effectively in those markets constitute a substantial barrier to liberalized trade in international air services.

Ancillary Market Restrictions

Competitive conditions in downstream or related markets can also impair the competitiveness of international air services markets. The existence of government-owned or sanctioned monopolies for the provision of airport facilities and services and for computerized reservations services has spawned serious disputes between the United States and Italy, France, Germany, and the United Kingdom. Foreign and some U.S. carriers have also questioned the market power of several large airline computerized reservations systems.

State Ownership and Subsidization

State subsidization of airlines may prove to be the most troublesome barrier to liberalized trade in air services because it discourages governments of state-subsidized and privately owned airlines from accepting greater liberalization. State ownership of airlines may pose difficult problems even when direct subsidies are not involved since governments that consider airlines to be instruments of national policy are often reluctant to expose their airlines to increased competition. For some, the concern is the survival of the national flag airline. For others, it is the maintenance of domestic controls that permits them to subsidize a national airline through higher passenger fares rather than budgetary appropriations.

Management and labor unions of state-owned airlines may also be less than enthusiastic about giving up the shelter of the state for the uncertainties of a more competitive marketplace. In addition, they are often skeptical that the government would permit them to abandon routes, reduce employment, lower wages, and take other steps necessary to compete in a more open trading system.

Privately owned airlines in the United States and abroad also question the willingness of most governments to eliminate subsidies and other supports for their national flag carriers. Thus, U.S. carriers have opposed liberalizing the access of foreign airlines on the grounds that permitting increased competition with such carriers is asking the U.S. industry to engage in a bleeding contest with a blood bank. Excluding foreign carriers from the U.S. domestic markets and restricting access to U.S. gateways are viewed as a type of countervailing protection against "unfair" competition from government-supported airlines.

U.S. INTERNATIONAL AIR SERVICES: A BRIEF HISTORY

Airline service is a relative newcomer to the international arena. The first international air services date back to the 1920s, but not until the postwar period did international air services attain economic significance. Prior to World War II, U.S. carriers negotiated directly with foreign governments—often in fierce competition with other U.S. airlines—for the rights to serve foreign territories. Although the Department of State sometimes assisted U.S. airlines to further American diplomatic interests (for example, Pan American in South America), only in 1943 did the U.S. government begin to assume responsibility for air service negotiations.

At the 1944 Chicago Conference on International Civil Aviation, the United States pressed for an open, multilateral regime for postwar international air services.[3] When the conference failed to reach accord on such an agreement, bilateral air services agreements became the basis for international air service operations. The U.S.-U.K. (Bermuda I) Agreement was the most common form of bilateral agreement and remains the intellectual foundation of air service bilateralism.

Changes in technology, demographics, and airline economics since 1945 have significantly altered the market for international air services. Aircraft technology bounded from DC-3s to 747s, from piston prop to jet turbine engines, from 30-passenger planes to 500-passenger widebodies. Moreover, the market for international air services experienced major economic and demographic changes. In the United States, population growth shifted from the Northeast and North Central states to the Sunbelt; high technology superseded shoes and textiles as New England's primary industry, while services overtook manufacturing in New York.

U.S. international aviation policy, however, remained substantially unchanged from the immediate post–World War II period, when the United States negotiated most of its international air services agreements, until 1978. Prices were subject to government approval, and a limited number of carriers enjoyed U.S. flag monopoly or duopoly status on international routes.

Routes were defined in the bilateral agreement. To accommodate aircraft range limitations and take maximum advantage of aircraft scale economies, international airlines have traditionally funneled traffic to gateway cities for connection to long-haul international sectors. An airline's ability to capture sufficient traffic at its gateways to support large, international-range aircraft became critical to its success on that route. U.S. agreements typically gave a foreign carrier access to one or two U.S. gateway cities, which the carrier could serve from any point in its home territory. In return, U.S. carriers received rights to serve several cities in the foreign nation from the United States.

Although national geography and traditional domestic transportation systems made it possible to serve many countries—including such major aviation powers as Great Britain and France—through one principal gateway, the geographic expanse of the United States, the population shift to the Sunbelt, and further advances in aircraft technology have all made effective access to multiple gateways essential for most foreign airlines serving the United States. Advances in aircraft and engine technology, combined with the development of hub-and-spoke networks by deregulated U.S. airlines, have permitted U.S. airlines to institute nonstop international air services from a host of new gateways (Dallas, Houston, Atlanta, St. Louis, Cincinnati, and Charlotte) with sufficient "behind gateway" services to collect the traffic needed to support economically viable international services. Bilateral route restrictions, however, have impeded foreign carrier access to these new gateways.

SERVICE INDUSTRY PARALLELS: SOME PRELIMINARY OBSERVATIONS

One of the difficult problems posed by broad-based service negotiations is the extent to which negotiators should deal with service issues generically or on an industry-specific basis. Existing domestic regulatory systems for most service industries suggest that an industry-specific focus will be the political reality. Yet the very restrictiveness of many domestic regulatory systems—particularly when coupled with the inherent limitations imposed by single-sector bargaining on the possibility of making mutually beneficial cross-sectoral trades—seems to compel a broader orientation if the service talks are ultimately to succeed.

In assessing the appropriate mix of industry-specific versus general focus for trade-in-service negotiations, it is useful to identify some important similarities across service industries. Three are particularly notable: the importance of networks, the threat of diversion, and privatization.

The Importance of Networks

The structure of airline services today reflects the increasing importance of networks in general. An airline hub diagram could just as easily illustrate a telecommunications network, a marine cargo transport system, or even a financial clearinghouse operation.

Networks permit firms to capture available economies of scale and scope and to meet user requirements better. This is particularly true for users with geographically dispersed operations or those otherwise requiring regular access to a variety of different locations. There is strong evidence that airline passengers and air cargo shippers prefer single-carrier service over service involving connections between carriers, and it appears that similar advantages from networks may accrue to other service industries as well. Chapter 2 describes the economics of a hub network. The existence of network economies also has important negotiating implications, as discussed in Chapters 6 and 7.

Deregulation and the Threat of Diversion

Air transport is one of several service industries that have been deregulated in a number of countries, including the United States, Canada, Japan, Australia, New Zealand, Great Britain, the People's Republic of China, and the European Economic Community (EEC). Similar developments have occurred in financial services where substantial deregulation has occurred in domestic capital markets as nations strive to remain competitive in global money market competition. The United Kingdom, for example, deregulated stock brokerage commissions on the London markets some eleven years after the United States took a similar step in 1975. The U.S. Congress and bank regulators are currently discussing a range of deregulatory measures aimed at making U.S. banks more competitive with their foreign and offshore counterparts.[4] Similar, but to date more limited, steps toward deregulation have been taken in foreign telecommunications services.[5]

The threat of diversion has made deregulation of service industries an attractive means of capturing markets. When the United States negotiated liberal aviation agreements with the Netherlands and Belgium, for example, airline passengers quickly discovered that they could avoid high fares to more restrictive countries by flying to Holland and entering the other countries via surface transportation. The threatened impact of traffic diversion from German and British airlines encouraged both governments to negotiate more liberal air service agreements with the United States. Similar competitive concerns have led to significant deregulation in other service industries, including financial services and telecommunications. The negotiating implications of deregulation and diversion are discussed in Chapters 4 and 6.

Privatization

Airlines, like many service industries, have been affected by the worldwide trend to privatize state-owned enterprises. In addition to the complete privatization of British Airways and the privatization of Japan Air Lines now under way, full or partial privatization is being actively considered for Air Canada, Air France, and Lufthansa (Germany), among others. The movement toward privatization of major international airlines could significantly increase the prospects of liberalized trade in air services. A reduction in the number of state-owned competitors could alleviate many difficult problems in air services markets, and possibly in other service sectors as well. Further, privatization could expand the core group of nations willing to liberalize air services. Chaper 7 presents strategy for building a liberal international regime for air services on a foundation of nations with deregulated airline markets and private airlines.

PERSPECTIVE

This book examines how trade in air services can be liberalized and what role, if any, multilateral service negotiations can play in the process. The following chapters consider the economic and political acceptability of liberalization for nations and the affected interest groups therein, as well as strategies for exploiting existing economic and political forces to liberalize the regime governing international air services.

NOTES

1. Bin Cheng, "The Case for a Multilateral Legal Framework for International Air Services," Trade Policy Research Centre, October 1982 uses the term *liberalization* somewhat differently and specifically excludes as liberalization "recent United States bilateral agreements, (which) deliberately and suddenly inject(ed) a massive dose of aggressive competition into the industry. . . ." In

this book, however, the term refers to changes in the prevailing air services regulatory regime that seek to increase competition, airline efficiency, and hence total welfare. Thus, the U.S. agreements excluded by Cheng are most certainly liberalizations as that term is used here.

2. The term *international air services* describes only those services connecting two or more national markets; it does not connote the carriage of purely domestic traffic by a foreign airline.
3. W. Pogue, "International Civil Air Transport—Transition Following WW II," Massachusetts Institute of Technology Report PTL-R79-6, June 1979.
4. I. Walter, *Global Competition in Financial Services: Market Structure, Protection, and Liberalization* (Cambridge, Mass.: Ballinger, 1988).
5. J. Aronson and P. Cowhey, *When Countries Talk: International Trade in Telecommunications Services* (Cambridge, Mass.: Ballinger, 1988).

2

THE WORLD MARKET FOR COMMERCIAL AIR SERVICES

Commercial airline services are provided on both a regularly scheduled and a charter basis. Scheduled services are provided over a specified route (for example, New York–London) on a regularly scheduled basis (such as daily) and are sold to the general public. Charter services are usually sold to another party, which must then fill the aircraft. A tour operator, for instance, might charter an aircraft to fly to Aruba. The operator then resells seats on the flight to vacationers, typically as part of a package that includes ground accommodations, local transfers, and so forth. (For those more familiar with the maritime industry, these categories roughly correspond to the distinction between liner and tramp services in ocean shipping.) Regularly scheduled airlines provide both scheduled and charter air services, while charter operators generally provide only charter services.

Charter and scheduled airlines provide both passenger and cargo services. All-cargo carriers, such as Flying Tigers, Cargolux, and Federal Express, use their fleets of freighter aircraft exclusively for carrying air cargo. Airlines such as American Airlines and Pan American offer combination services; that is, they operate no freighter aircraft, instead concentrating principally on passenger markets, but do carry cargo in the belly holds of their passenger aircraft. Other predominantly passenger airlines, such as Lufthansa and Northwest, operate both freighter and passenger aircraft, enabling them to provide cargo capacity beyond that available in the bellies of passenger aircraft.

Scheduled air services account for the predominant share of total airline traffic. In 1986 approximately 91 percent of all airline traffic is measured in revenue tonne kilometers (RTKs) and 90 percent of world passenger traffic as measured in revenue passenger kilometers (RPKs) was carried on scheduled airline services (see Table 2–1). (An RPK is one revenue passenger carried one kilometer.)

Scheduled airlines carried some 950 million passengers over 1,442 billion kilometers in 1986. Scheduled carriers also moved 14.7 million tonnes of air cargo more than 43,210 tonne-kilometers (one tonne carried one kilometer) during that same period. Passengers and their baggage accounted for 73 percent of the total RTKs generated by scheduled airlines, with freight and mail contributing the remainder. Passenger revenues provided an even higher proportion of total scheduled service revenues, amounting to 78.1 percent in 1985. Tables 2–2 and 2–3 show the recent growth of scheduled airline traffic, revenues, and expenses.

Domestic passenger traffic accounted for 54 percent of the world's total passenger traffic. Domestic scheduled passenger traffic constituted more than 58 percent of total scheduled passenger traffic (measured in RPKs) and more than 79 percent in terms of the number of passengers. Domestic air cargo traffic carried on scheduled services constituted only 28.5 percent of the total air freight (measured in RTKs) carried on scheduled services, but made up more than 56 percent measured in tons.

Table 2–1. Percentage Distribution of World Airline Traffic by Type of Service, 1986.

	International	*Domestic*	*Total*
All services (in RTKs)			
Scheduled	85.8	97.2	91.2
Charter	14.2	2.8	8.8
Passenger services (in RPKs)			
Scheduled	82.1	98.2	90.1
Charter	17.9	1.8	9.9

Source: International Air Transport Association, *World Air Transport Statistics, 1986* (Montreal: IATA, 1987).

REGIONAL DISTRIBUTION OF TRAFFIC

The United States and Canada accounted for 58 percent of all domestic scheduled airline traffic in 1985, a share that has increased slightly over the past decade. This gain reflects the dramatic growth in domestic U.S. traffic spurred by deregulation of the U.S. domestic airline market. European airlines captured the largest share of international scheduled airline traffic, but Asian and Pacific airlines are making rapid gains. North America ranks third in the percentage of scheduled international traffic (measured in RTKs).

Due to substantial differences in the physical size and geography of nations, flight distances that would be international in Europe are domestic in the United States and Canada. Thus, a combination of domestic and international data is a better measure of market share. Airlines from the United States and Canada carry more than 38 percent of all scheduled airline traffic, followed by European carriers with almost 33 percent and Asian and Pacific carriers with almost 18 percent. Table 2–4 shows the regional distribution of scheduled airline traffic for 1976 and 1985.

The North Atlantic market is by far the largest international passenger market in the world; the intra-Europe market is a distant second. In 1985 the North Atlantic market accounted for 28 percent of all international passenger kilometers, while intra-Europe services accounted for 12 percent. Figure 2–1 shows worldwide international passenger flows.

THE WORLD AIRLINE INDUSTRY

An Overview

According to the International Air Transport Association, more than 300 airlines operated scheduled air services in 1986. This large number of airlines, however, does not accurately reflect the structure of the world airline industry. In reality, a

Table 2–2. World Air Transport Operations, 1976–1986.

International and Domestic Combined Traffic	Percent Change over Previous Year				1986 Preliminary Figures		Average Annual Changes		Total Change 1976–1986
	1982	1983	1984	1985	Number	Percent Change	1976–1986	1981–1986	
Scheduled Services									
Passengers carried (*thousands*)	2	4	6	6	949,900	6	5	5	65%
Freight tonnes carried (*thousands*)	6	6	9	2	14,700	7	5	6	57%
Passenger-kilometres flown (*millions*)	2	4	7	7	1,442,000	5	7	5	87%
Available seat-kilometres (*millions*)	2	3	6	5	2,213,000	6	6	5	74%
Passenger load factor (%)	—	1	1	1	65%	–1	1		5 pts
Tonne-kilometres performed (*millions*)									
Passenger (*incl. baggage*)	2	4	7	7	130,300	6	7	5	—
Freight (*incl. express*)	2	11	13	1	43,210	8	7	7	99%
Mail	2	3	8	2	4,490	2	4	3	45%
Total	2	6	9	5	178,000	6	7	6	89%
Available tonne-kilometres (*millions*)	2	3	8	5	297,010	7	6	5	—
Weight load factor (%)		1	1		60%	—			—
Charter Services of Scheduled Airlines									
Passenger-kilometres flown (*millions*)	—	–4	5	17	72,560	29	3	9	
Tonne-kilometres performed (*millions*)	–8	–3	6	17	9,110	31	4	8	
Available tonne-kilometres (*millions*)	–6	–3	5	19	13,670	23	4	7	

All Services of Scheduled Airlines								
Passenger-kilometres flown (*millions*)	2	4	7	7	1,514,560	6	6	5
Tonne-kilometres performed (*millions*)	2	5	9	6	187,110	7	7	6
Available tonne-kilometres (*millions*)	2	3	7	6	310,680	7	6	5
All Services of Charter Airlines								
Passenger-kilometres flown (*millions*)	15	8	6	1	73,570	6	2	5
Tonne-kilometres performed (*millions*)	15	5	8	3	8,080	–10	1	4
Available tonne-kilometres (*millions*)	15	—	7	4	11,090	–6	1	4
Total Charter Services								
Passenger-kilometres flown (*millions*)	8	3	6	7	146,130	8	3	7
Tonne-kilometres performed (*millions*)	4	1	7	9	17,190	8	3	6
Available tonne-kilometres (*millions*)	4	–1	6	10	24,760	8	2	5
All Services of all Commercial Airlines								
Passenger-kilometres flown (*millions*)	3	4	7	7	1,588,130	6	6	5
Tonne-kilometres performed (*millions*)	2	5	9	6	195,190	6	6	6
Available tonne-kilometres (*millions*)	2	3	7	6	321,770	7	5	5

Conversion factors to metric units are as follows: 1 short ton (2,000 lbs.)= 0.9072 tonnes; 1 long ton (2,240 lbs.) = 1.0160 tonnes; 1 statute mile (5,280 ft.) = 1.6093 kilometers; 1 ton-mile (short tons and statute miles) = 1.4600 tonne-kilometers; 1 ton-mile (long tons and statute miles) = 1.6352 tonne-kilometers.

Source: International Air Transport Association, *World Air Transport Statistics, 1986* (Montreal: IATA, 1987); International Civil Aviation Organization.

Table 2–3. Operating Revenues and Expenses of World Scheduled Airlines Calendar Years 1980–1985 ($ U.S. Millions).[a]

	1980	*1981*	*1982*	*1983[b]*	*1984*	*1985[c]*	*1980–85*
Operating Revenues							
Scheduled Services							
Passenger	$69,930	$74,433	$74,860	$77,600	$ 81,350	$ 87,500	25.1%
Freight	9,468	9,523	9,560	10,830	12,450	12,500	32.0
Mail	1,501	1,425	1,480	1,470	1,500	1,500	—
Total Schedule Services	$80,899	$85,381	$85,900	$89,900	$ 95,300	$101,500	25.5
Nonscheduled Services	3,149	3,682	3,100	2,800	2,900	3,400	07.9
Incidental	3,628	3,929	4,240	5,600	6,600	7,100	95.7
Total Operating Revenues	$87,676	$92,992	$93,240	$98,300	$104,800	$112,000	27.8
Percentage Change	*	6.1	0.03	5.4	6.6	6.9	
Operating Expenses							
Total Operating Expenses	$88,310	$93,684	$93,400	$96,200	$ 99,700	$108,000	23.0
Percentage Change	*	6.1	(0.03)	3.0	3.6	8.3	
Operating Result	$ (635)	$ (692)	$ (160)	$ 2,100	$ 5,100	$ 4,000	
Percent of Revenue	(0.7)	(0.7)	(0.2)	2.1	4.9	3.6	
Net Result[d]	$ (919)	$(1,150)	$(1,300)	$ (700)	$ 2,000	NA[e]	
Percent of Revenue	(1.0)	(1.2)	(1.4)	(0.7)	1.9	NA[e]	

Note: Data in parentheses represent negative values.

a. Excludes domestic operations in the USSR.

b. Revised.

c. Preliminary.

d. Net Result equals Operating Result minus nonoperating items, including interest, income taxes, retirement of property and equipment, and affiliated companies and subsidies.

e. NA = Not available.

Source: International Civil Aviation Organization.

Figure 2–1. Percentage of Total International Passenger Kilometers, 1986.

Figure underneath stars is % of total/pax km within the region.

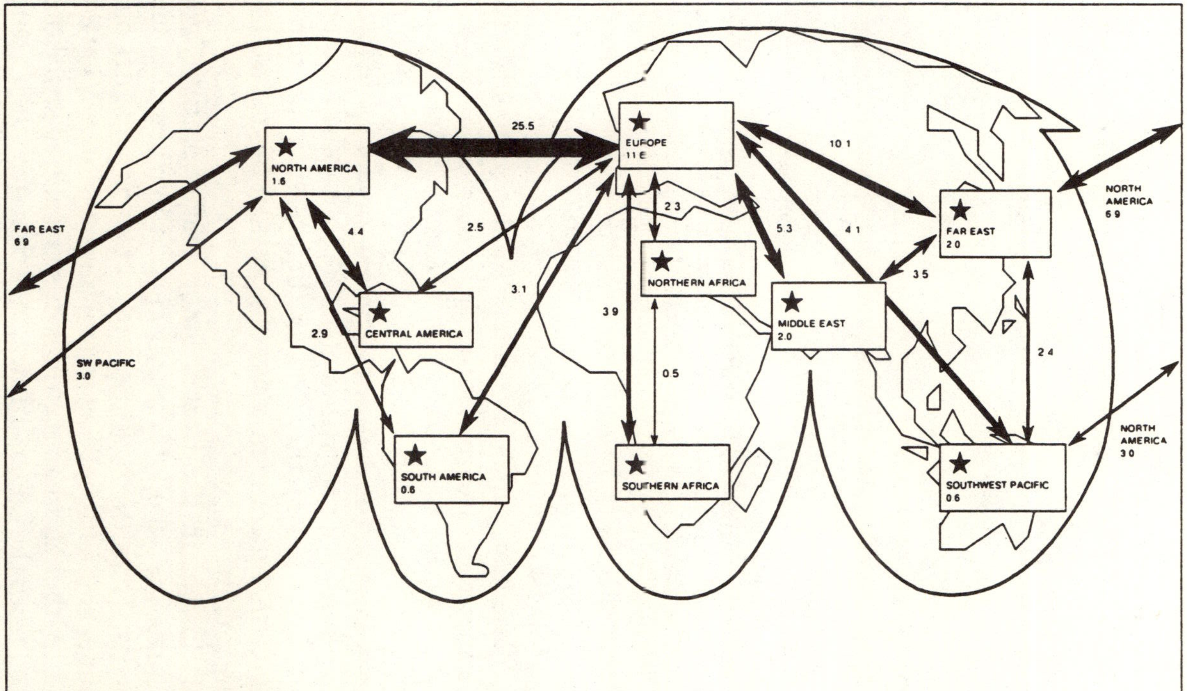

Source: IATA World Air Transport Statistics, 1986.

Table 2–4. Regional Distribution of Scheduled Traffic, 1985 and 1976.

Percentage of Total Ton-Kilometers	*All Services* 1976	*All Services* 1985	*International* 1976	*International* 1985	*Domestic* 1976	*Domestic* 1985
North America[a]	41.0	38.5	21.2	19.9	57.3	58.0
United States	37.8	37.9	—	—	—	—
Europe	36.5	32.7	42.9	37.5	31.2	27.6
Asia and Pacific	12.4	17.7	19.6	26.7	6.5	8.3
Latin America and Caribbean	4.8	4.9	6.4	5.7	3.5	4.1
Middle East	2.8	3.5	5.5	5.9	0.6	1.0
Africa	2.5	2.7	4.4	4.3	0.9	1.0
ICAO world	100	100	100	100	100	100

a. Canada and the United States only.

Sources: International Civil Aviation Organization; Aerospace Industries Association of America, *Aerospace Facts and Figures, 1986–1987* (Washington, D.C.: AIAA, 1987).

small number of big airlines generate most of the revenue passenger kilometers and ton-miles.

The top ranks of airlines in the noncommunist world, whether measured by traffic or revenue kilometers, are dominated by airlines based in North America and Western Europe. The relative size of world airlines reflects, among other things, the relative size and development of domestic markets, the distribution of international traffic flows, the development and sophistication of the airlines themselves, and market access problems inherent in a world governed by bilateral air service agreements.

Except in the United States and, recently, Great Britain, airlines are wholly or partly owned by their national governments. Thus, these airlines often enjoy monopolies on domestic routes and national flag monopolies on international routes.

Although smaller airlines historically acquired their aircraft used from the larger airlines, in recent years heightened competition for new aircraft sales, subsidized export financing, and the desire to build national airlines have motivated many national airlines to purchase new commercial aircraft.

U.S. Position in the World Airline Industry

U.S. airlines command the largest single share of world airline traffic—37.9 percent in 1985. Table 2–5 compares the changes in U.S. carrier market shares with changes in the U.S. share of world gross domestic product (GDP). From 1976 to 1985 the U.S. share of scheduled airline passenger traffic increased slightly and exceeded the U.S. share of world GDP, while the U.S. share of scheduled air freight markets declined and was lower than the U.S. shares of passenger traffic and of world GDP.

Despite the relative maturity of U.S. air services markets and the impact of the most severe economic recession since the 1930s, the U.S. airline industry exhibited strong growth over the decade from 1976 through 1986: passengers +87 percent; RPMs +105 percent; load factor +5 points; freight and express RTMs +44 percent; passenger revenues +181 percent; and freight and express revenues +276 percent. Table 2–6 provides year-by-year performance data for that period.

Table 2–5. U.S. Market Share, 1976 and 1985.

	Percent of Scheduled Cargo RTMs	*Percent of Scheduled Passenger RTMs*	*Percent of World GDP (current $)*
1976	32.7	37.6	38.5
1985	26.2	39.8	36.7

Sources: International Civil Aviation Organization; U.S. Department of Transportation, Office of Aviation Information Management, 1986; Air Transport Association Annual Reports, 1976–86; World Bank, *World Development Report 1987* (Washington, D.C.: World Bank, 1987).

Table 2–6. Selected Data for U.S. Scheduled Airlines, 1976–1986.[a]

	1976	*1977*	*1978*	*1979*
Traffic—Scheduled Service				
Revenue passengers enplaned (000)[b]	223,318	240,326	274,719	316,863
Revenue passenger miles (000)[c]	178,988,026	193,218,819	226,781,368	262,023,375
Available seat miles (000)[d]	322,821,649	345,565,901	368,750,530	416,126,429
Revenue passenger load factor (%)[e]	55.4	55.9	61.5	63.0
Average passenger trip length (miles)	801	804	826	827
Freight and express ton miles (000)[fg]	5,096,196	5,426,546	5,819,708	5,963,925
Aircraft departures	4,832,664	4,936,519	5,013,169	5,399,652
Passenger revenue ($000)	14,265,947	16,273,355	18,806,247	22,791,390
Freight and express revenues ($000)	1,497,123	1,718,529	1,986,820	2,211,321
Mail revenue ($000)	320,121	390,762	386,639	452,021
Charter revenue ($000)	572,580	644,381	578,285	520,916
Total operating revenues ($000)	17,501,215	19,924,800	22,883,955	27,226,665
Total operating expenses ($000)	16,779,282	19,016,760	21,519,092	27,026,610
Operating profit ($000)	721,933	908,040	1,364,863	199,055
Interest expense ($000)	371,634	373,206	538,642	618,446
Net profit ($000)	563,354	752,536	1,196,537	346,845
Revenue per passenger mile (¢)	8.0	8.4	8.3	8.7
Rate of return on investment (%)	8.5	10.2	13.3	6.5
Operating profit margin (%)[h]	4.1	4.6	6.0	0.7
Net profit margin (%)[i]	3.2	3.8	5.2	1.3
Employees	303,006	308,068	329,303	340,696

a. U.S. scheduled airlines are carriers certificated by the federal government under Section 401 of the Federal Aviation Act permitting the operation of large aircraft. Federal Express began reporting as a Section 401 carrier in 1986 and is included in 1986 data only.

b. The total number of revenue passengers boarding aircraft in scheduled service, including originating, stopover, or connecting passengers.

c. One fare-paying passenger transported one mile.

d. One seat transported one mile.

e. The percentage of seating or freight capacity that is utilized.

f. One ton of revenue traffic (passengers and cargo) transported one mile.

1980	*1981*	*1982*	*1983*	*1984*	*1985*	*1986*
296,903	285,976	294,102	318,638	344,683	382,022	418,493
255,192,114	248,887,801	259,643,870	281,829,148	305,115,855	336,403,021	366,283,158
432,535,103	424,897,230	440,119,206	464,537,979	515,323,339	547,788,432	606,847,601
59.0	58.6	59.0	60.7	59.2	61.4	60.4
860	870	883	884	885	881	875
5,741,567	5,686,087	5,482,198	6,092,932	6,566,571	6,030,543	7,335,942
5,352,927	5,211,867	4,963,794	5,033,906	5,448,150	5,835,474	6,415,110
28,048,689	30,722,629	30,549,719	32,744,618	36,939,345	39,235,809	40,056,093
2,431,926	2,596,850	2,437,703	2,592,567	2,859,419	2,680,715	5,627,996
610,996	653,996	688,675	653,129	712,070	889,575	838,278
1,160,524	1,175,154	1,085,537	1,076,428	1,112,050	1,279,812	1,268,899
33,727,806	36,662,555	36,407,635	38,953,672	43,825,047	46,664,414	50,524,933
33,949,421	37,117,325	37,141,070	38,643,262	41,673,536	45,238,150	49,201,832
(221,615)	(454,770)	(733,435)	310,410	2,151,511	1,426,264	1,323,101
967,719	1,209,461	1,384,084	1,482,352	1,540,377	1,588,306	1,692,548
17,414	(300,826)	(915,814)	(188,051)	824,668	862,715	(234,909)
11.0	12.3	11.8	11.6	12.1	11.7	10.8
5.3	4.7	2.1	6.0	9.9	9.6	5.2
(0.7)	(1.2)	(2.0)	0.8	4.9	3.1	2.6
0.1	(0.8)	(2.5)	(0.5)	1.9	1.8	(0.5)
360,517	349,864	330,495	328,648	345,079	355,113	421,686

g. Air cargo means the total volume of freight, mail, and express traffic transported by air. Statistics are given for (1) freight and express commodities of all kinds, including small package counter services, express services, and priority reserved freight, and (2) all classes of mail transported for the U.S. Postal Service.

h. Operating profit (operating revenues minus operating expenses) as percent of operating revenues.

i. Net profit after interest and after taxes as percent of operating revenues.

Source: Air Transport Association Annual Report, 1987, Washington, D.C.

Passenger Services. U.S. carriers dominated the list of the world's largest passenger airlines in 1986 (see Table 2–7). This reflects the large absolute and relative size of the U.S. domestic air services market and, to a lesser extent, the size of U.S. international air service markets.

The United States enjoyed a strong, but not predominant, position in its international passenger markets. Table 2–8 shows that U.S. carriers in aggregate have maintained roughly a 50 percent share of the international passenger traffic to and from the United States since 1975, despite sometimes significant changes in shares for specific countries and regions.

Commercial airline passenger traffic between the United States and foreign countries (excluding Canada) amounted to slightly more than 46.5 million passengers in 1985. The North Atlantic market (that is, routes between the United States and Europe) was by far the largest market, accounting for some 41 percent of all U.S. international passenger traffic (see Table 2–9).

Historically, variations in U.S. carrier market share have coincided with changes in the citizenship composition of the traffic pool, rising when the proportion of U.S. citizens increased and falling as the percentage of U.S. citizens declined.

Table 2–7. Top Ranking Scheduled Airlines, 1986.

Carrier	*RPKs (Millions)*
1. Texas Air	114,634
2. United	95,350
3. American	82,101
4. Delta	68,133
5. Northwest	58,133
6. TWA	47,629
7. USAir	41,487
8. British Airways	40,430
9. Japan Air Lines	38,511

Sources: U.S. Department of Transportation, and International Air Transport Association, *World Air Transport Statistics, 1986* (Montreal: IATA, 1987).

Table 2–8. U.S. Market Shares of Scheduled and Charter Passenger Traffic between the United States and Region or Country (percent).

Region or Country	*1975*	*1976*	*1977*	*1978*	*1979*	*1980*	*1981*	*1982*	*1983*	*1984*	*1985*
All countries	50.26	50.34	50.43	50.02	50.84	49.09	48.65	49.69	50.75	49.43	48.20
Central America and Mexico	58.55	56.18	55.49	56.14	57.48	53.98	55.77	52.58	48.61	43.56	41.80
Caribbean	63.92	64.84	66.96	68.55	68.34	69.20	69.93	70.91	72.06	69.34	66.20
South America	43.27	38.99	41.29	44.06	44.87	44.56	43.91	41.73	41.97	38.20	36.60
Europe	44.04	45.36	45.40	43.94	44.22	42.08	40.99	44.91	46.52	47.22	47.22
France	40.44	44.75	51.61	51.91	51.56	49.02	48.03	50.37	52.36	54.32	57.40
West Germany	43.16	50.49	49.12	44.44	45.30	50.63	46.44	47.17	46.75	47.50	54.90
Italy	60.70	61.27	59.28	58.76	61.57	56.72	56.10	59.88	61.46	61.59	58.30
Netherlands	14.21	8.62	8.63	11.61	23.39	12.25	7.31	5.68	2.86	7.45	9.10
United Kingdom	57.80	56.86	55.54	53.41	52.57	47.80	49.97	58.31	61.81	60.84	56.60
Africa	74.39	68.14	64.74	58.17	47.30	42.58	39.27	42.95	47.98	51.91	36.70
Middle East	25.43	15.96	22.30	21.90	26.52	34.52	34.94	34.79	37.70	38.63	40.30
Far East	41.01	45.10	43.71	41.32	44.25	41.38	39.01	39.29	41.40	42.57	41.00
Hong Kong	75.58	79.57	77.26	76.50	80.04	70.71	68.93	61.16	60.60	59.34	56.10
Japan	40.48	45.16	46.25	43.23	46.23	44.53	40.44	42.85	47.00	48.08	47.80
Oceania	52.42	49.27	49.85	46.56	50.90	48.17	48.59	45.44	45.56	44.77	43.80

Source: U.S. Department of Transportation, *U.S. International Air Travel Statistics* (Cambridge, Mass., 1975–86).

Table 2–9. U.S. International Passenger Traffic, 1985.

Region	*Passengers (000,000)*	*Share (%)*
All countries	46.6	100.0
Central America and Mexico	6.8	14.6
Caribbean	8.8	18.9
South America	2.4	5.2
Europe	19.0	40.7
Africa/Middle East	1.1	2.4
Far East	7.0	15.0
Oceania	1.5	3.2

Source: U.S. Department of Transportation, *U.S. International Air Travel Statistics* (Cambridge, Mass., 1986).

The United States also showed strength in, but not dominance of, individual airline market shares in specific international markets. In the North Atlantic, for instance, two U.S. airlines ranked in the top five passenger airlines, three in the top ten, and five in the top fifteen providing service between the United States and Europe (see Table 2–10).

Charters carried about 6 percent of all international passengers traveling to and from the United States in 1986. Of these charter passengers, U.S. carriers carried 54 percent. Prior to the introduction of low-fare scheduled service across the North Atlantic, charters carried as much as 27 percent of the passenger traffic in that market. Table 2–11 shows the distribution of U.S. international passenger traffic between scheduled and charter services for the period 1976 through 1986.

Freight Service. The United States held a large but diminishing share of the total world air cargo market in 1986. Nonetheless, U.S. airlines occupied five of the top ten positions among the world's largest cargo airlines, and six of the top fifteen positions (see Table 2–12).

With the exceptions of Flying Tigers and Northwest, however, the U.S. strength comes largely from cargo carriage in the U.S. domestic market. Thus, if international tonne-kilometers

Table 2–10. Top Fifteen Airlines Flying across the North Atlantic, 1986.

Airline	*Passengers (in thousands)*	*Market Share (percent)*
1. Pan Am	2,601	12.3
2. TWA	2,401	11.4
3. British Airways	2,005	9.5
4. Lufthansa	1,348	6.4
5. KLM	1,143	5.4
6. Air Canada	863	4.1
7. Air France	725	3.4
8. Swissair	603	2.9
9. Northwest	577	2.7
10. Alitalia	575	2.7
11. SAS	529	2.5
12. American	524	2.5
13. British Caledonian	475	2.3
14. People	433	2.1
15. Iberia	417	2.0
Top fifteen total	15,219	72.2
Total North Atlantic	21,083	100.0

Source: International Air Transport Association, *North Atlantic Passenger Traffic Report* (Montreal: IATA, 1987).

Table 2–11. Percent Distribution of U.S. International Passenger Traffic, 1976–1986.

	Scheduled		*Charter*	
	Total	*Europe*	*Total*	*Europe*
1976	84	75	16	25
1977	83	73	17	27
1978	87	81	13	19
1979	90	87	10	13
1980	93	91	7	9
1981	94	94	6	6
1982	93	91	7	9
1983	92	90	8	10
1984	92	91	8	9
1985	93	92	7	8
1986	94	95	6	5

Source: U.S. Department of Transportation, *U.S. International Travel Statistics* (Cambridge, Mass., 1976–86).

Table 2–12. 1986 Rankings by Scheduled Freight Tonne-Kilometers Performed.

International			*Domestic*			*Total*		
Rank	*Airline*	*Millions*	*Rank*	*Airline*	*Millions*	*Rank*	*Airline*	*Millions*
1.	Lufthansa	2,793	1.	Flying Tigers	1,265	1.	Flying Tigers	3,099
2.	Japan Air Lines	2,661	2.	Federal Express	1,141	3.	Japan Air Lines	2,834
3.	Air France	2,501	3.	United Airlines	699	3.	Lufthansa	2,816
4.	Flying Tigers	1,834	4.	Eastern Air Lines	388	4.	Air France	2,632
5.	KLM	1,497	5.	American Airlines	340	5.	KLM	1,497
6.	British Airways	1,241	6.	Northwest	300[a]	6.	Northwest	1,468
7.	Northwest	1,168[a]	7.	Delta	300[a]	7.	British Airways	1,244
8.	Alitalia	818	8.	TWA	221	8.	Federal Express	1,218
9.	Pan American	745	9.	VARIG	201	9.	United Airlines	1,004
10.	Qantas Airways	729	10.	Continental Airlines	196	10.	Alitalia	842
11.	Swissair	666	11.	Air Canada	187	11.	Pan American	839
12.	Sabena	574	12.	Japan Air Lines	173	12.	VARIG	752
13.	El Al	571	13.	Air France	131	13.	Qantas Airways	729
14.	VARIG	551	14.	Transbrasil	107	14.	Swissair	674
15.	Iberia	468	15.	Pan American	94	15.	Air Canada	648

a. Estimate.

Sources: International Air Transport Association, *World Air Transport Statistics, 1986* (Montreal: IATA, 1987); *U.S. Air Transport Association Annual Report, 1987* (Washington, D.C., June 1987).

are considered, only three U.S. carriers ranked in the top ten international air freight carriers.

Over the past decade, the U.S. air cargo industry has witnessed the explosive growth of the small package express (next-day delivery) business, while the traditional air cargo business has remained relatively flat. While air freight worldwide grew at an average annual rate of 8 percent from 1976 to 1986,[1] small-package express growth rates over that same period ranged from 70 percent per year in the mid-1970s to approximately 20 percent per year in 1986.[2]

Since small packages and documents cost more per pound to ship than does standard air freight, the growth in air freight revenues outstripped the growth in air freight tonnage, the traditional measure of air cargo market share (Table 2–13).

Aggressive international expansion initiated in recent years by U.S. small-package carriers, including Federal Express, United Parcel Service (UPS), and Emery, puts U.S. carriers in a strong position to dominate the emerging international small-package express markets. Based on the anticipated growth of the international market for package express services, the United States could thus find its position in the air freight market strengthened over the next several years.

THE IMPACT OF U.S. AIRLINE DEREGULATION

From the passage of the Civil Aeronautics Act in 1938 until enactment of the Airline Deregulation Act of 1978, the U.S. Civil Aeronautics Board (CAB) regulated U.S. domestic airlines like public utilities—strictly limiting competition by controlling entry, pricing, and route selection. Once they obtained operating authority, carriers effectively enjoyed franchises to serve certain specified markets but not others. Both actual and potential competition were strictly limited. Prices were set on the basis of overall industry profitability rather than by the relationship

Table 2–13. U.S. Scheduled Airlines Growth in Cargo Tonnage and Revenues.

	1976	*1986*	*Total Increase*
Freight and express RTMs (000)	5,096,196	7,335,942	44%
Freight and express revenue (000)	$1,497,123	$5,627,996	276%

between fares and costs in specific markets. Although the Civil Aeronautics Act did not preclude price competition, in practice the CAB severely constrained such competition.[3]

As the trunk airlines—those initially licensed by the CAB in the late 1930s—gradually acquired larger, longer range aircraft (upgrading from DC-3s to DC-6s and Constellations to B-707s, DC-8s, etc.), the CAB permitted these carriers to serve the types of longer haul routes better suited to the new aircraft. It then authorized "feeder" airlines to serve the shorter routes abandoned by the trunks with other smaller capacity equipment no longer utilized by the trunks. Over time, as these feeders acquired larger equipment and routes, the CAB permitted third-level carriers to provide air taxi service over routes, such as Harrisburg-Pittsburgh, that were too small for (or otherwise unserved by) the larger airlines. Today's U.S. commuter airlines are the direct descendants of those third-level carriers.

The CAB integrated the three levels of service into a national air transportation system by awarding routes to trunks and feeders. Third-level carriers operating small aircraft were generally exempt from CAB route and rate regulation. The overall scheme was to have trunks carry the vast majority of the traffic on their services between major traffic generating points. Second-level carriers would take passengers traveling to or from smaller cities from those points into the trunk system. Third-level carriers were to fill the remaining service gaps.

Historically, the trunk airlines have dominated the U.S. airline industry. For most of the 1970s, eleven trunks collectively held 88 percent or more of the U.S. domestic passenger market. Although the CAB sometimes permitted two carriers to serve the same route, most routes were monopolized by a single carrier. Most U.S. airlines had, in reality, an economically inefficient crazy quilt of route rights. Only United Airlines' route structure was extensive enough to approach a truly national status.

Trunks also dominated the U.S. international market. Pan American operated exclusively international services and held virtually worldwide operating authority. Three others held international authority (not including transborder services to Canada and Mexico): TWA flew to a number of destinations in Europe; Northwest flew to Japan and points in Asia; and Braniff flew to Latin America. International traffic accounted for about 10 percent of the total passenger traffic carried by U.S. airlines.

The passage of the Airline Deregulation Act of 1978 (ADA) ended the CAB's forty-year reign.[4] For air cargo, deregulation came a year earlier. The ADA dismantled the system of economic regulation under which U.S. airlines had operated, explicitly leaving regulation of the industry to the forces of marketplace competition. (Regulation of safety matters was retained under the U.S. Federal Aviation Administration.)

The elimination of entry, pricing, route, and other restrictions that had prevented or impaired competition in U.S. domestic airline markets transformed the U.S. air transportation industry. Freed of CAB control, airlines radically realigned their route structures, explored dramatically new pricing strategies, adjusted their aircraft fleets, developed a range of new competitive weapons including computerized reservations systems and frequent flier programs, and consummated a rash of mergers and acquisitions. Several of the more significant changes precipitated by deregulation are examined below.[5]

Route Systems

Deregulation prompted a series of changes in U.S. airline route structures and service patterns. Perhaps the most dramatic change has been the rapid growth of hub-and-spoke operations. Table 2–14 shows the sharp increase in hubbing during the first five years after deregulation.

Hubbing is a process by which an airline operates connecting banks of arriving and departing flights at selected airports. Hubbing thus allows passengers and cargo to move conveniently to connecting flights at the hub with a minimum of delay. By channeling passengers from many points through an intermediate connecting point, or hub, a carrier can combine passengers with different origins and destinations and thereby increase the number of city-pairs served (see Figure 2–2) as well as the average number of passengers and revenue per flight.

TWA's operations at St. Louis' Lambert International Airport provide an excellent example of the economic advantages of hubbing. Figure 2–3 is a flight matrix extracted from TWA's schedule at the St. Louis hub that illustrates the connecting bank of flights moving through the hub and on to their final destinations. By scheduling banks of arriving and departing flights within a short time span, TWA maximized the number of connecting flights, and hence services, available to its customers. Flight 155, for instance, provided on-line connections from Chicago to thirty-three destinations.

The elimination of government restrictions on airline entry and route selection, coupled with the underlying economics of hub-and-spoke operations, has heightened the necessity of ensuring sufficient traffic to support the operations. To increase the effectiveness of their hubs and to offer a wide array of on-line services to attract customers, U.S. airlines have aggressively sought new traffic sources. They have increased the number of flights out of existing hubs; established new hubs in areas such

Table 2–14. The Growth of Hubbing.

Airline	Leading Hub City in 1983	Percent of Airline's Domestic Departures at Hub 1978	Percent of Airline's Domestic Departures at Hub 1983	Percent Change in Departures at Hub
American	Dallas-Ft. Worth	11.2	28.6	113.7
Continental[a]	Houston	12.8	22.9	45.8
Delta	Atlanta	18.3	21.4	11.4
Eastern	Atlanta	18.3	21.0	1.0
Frontier	Denver	18.0	33.8	23.8
Northwest[b]	Minneapolis-St. Paul	16.1	20.7	18.7
Ozark	St. Louis	15.5	35.6	53.7
Pan American[c]	New York	12.3	22.4	–1.8
Piedmont	Charlotte	3.7	19.6	583.0
Republic[d]	Minneapolis-St. Paul	3.4	7.7	91.1
TWA	St. Louis	11.9	33.0	81.3
United	Chicago	13.8	18.9	1.5
USAir	Pittsburgh	16.0	23.2	45.7
Western	Salt Lake City	10.3	16.9	129.3

a. Continental and Texas International departures are combined for 1978.

b. There was a strike at Northwest in the second quarter of 1978; therefore, in both years data for service during the first quarter are reported.

c. National and Pan American departures are combined for 1978.

d. North Central, Southern, and Hughes Airwest departures are combined for 1978.

Source: Service Segment Data taken from CAB Report to Congress, *Implementation of the Provisions of the Airline Deregulation Act of 1978* (Washington, D.C., January 31, 1984).

as Salt Lake City, Nashville, Raleigh-Durham, and Cincinnati; acquired other airlines with existing hub-and-spoke operations; and acquired effective control over regional airlines that serve the smaller routes to and from the major carrier hubs. As shown in Table 2–15, the result has been a substantial increase in the percentage of air travelers who fly their complete journey on-line

Figure 2–2. Leverage of Hub Connections.

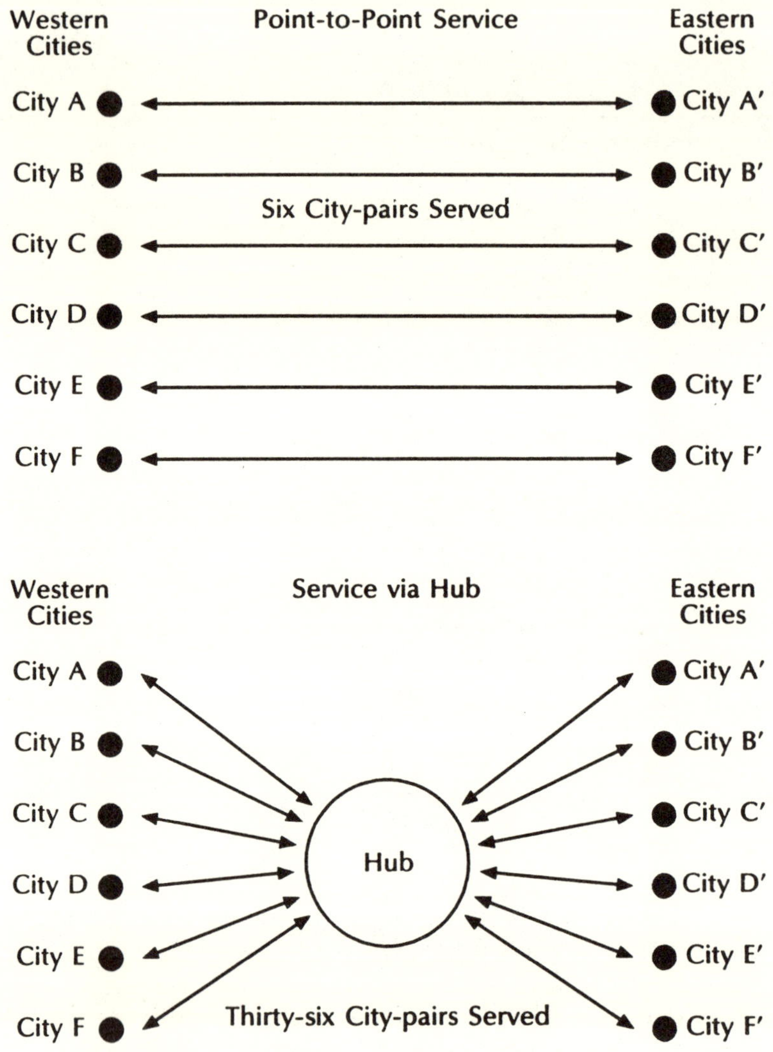

Figure 2–3. Matrix of TWA Flight Connections through Its St. Louis Hub.

		St. Louis Hub			
Flight	*Origin*	*Arrive*	*Connect with*	*Depart*	*Destination*
155	Chicago				
	9:45 AM	10:48 AM	7011	11:30 AM	Lake of the Ozarks
			7045	11:35 AM	Springfield, MO
			7023	11:35 AM	Columbia, MO
			7053	11:40 AM	Joplin
			419	11:45 AM	Las Vegas
			123	11:50 AM	Albuquerque
			561	11:50 AM	Denver
			131	11:50 AM	Oklahoma City
			509	11:50 AM	Phoenix
			155	11:50 AM	Tucson
			27	11:50 AM	Tulsa
			489	11:55 AM	Little Rock
			273	12:00 NOON	Colorado Springs
			91	12:00 NOON	Los Angeles
			221	12:00 NOON	San Antonio
			177	12:00 NOON	San Francisco
			405	12:00 NOON	Wichita
			451	12:05 PM	Austin
			451	12:05 PM	Dallas/Ft. Worth
			525	12:05 PM	Houston
			259	12:05 PM	Omaha
			245	12:05 PM	Salt Lake City
			7032	1:15 PM	Carbondale, IL
			335	1:16 PM	Des Moines
			168	1:30 PM	Atlanta
			20	1:30 PM	Nassau/Freeport
			528	1:30 PM	Pittsburgh
			892	1:30 PM	Washington National
			208	1:45 PM	Memphis
			406	1:45 PM	Nashville
			590	1:50 PM	Baltimore
			30	1:55 PM	Louisville
			18	1:55 PM	San Juan, PR

Source: *TWA Flight Guide*, October 1–26, 1985.

Table 2–15. The Decline of Interlining on U.S. Domestic Scheduled Services (percent).

	On-Line	*Interline*
1973	77.1	22.9
1974	76.7	23.2
1975	76.4	23.6
1976	76.0	24.0
1977	75.4	24.6
1978	76.8	23.2
1979	78.9	21.1
1980	81.9	18.1
1981	84.6	15.4
1982	87.1	12.9
1983	89.1	10.9
1984	89.6	10.4

Source: U.S. Department of Transportation, "Interline Practices in the Airline Industry," January 1986.

(that is, on a single airline). Concomitantly, the percentage of travelers interlining between airlines has declined.

Computerized Ticketing and Reservations Systems

The proliferation of, and rapid changes in, fare types, levels, and conditions since deregulation has immensely complicated the task of marketing airline services. One result has been the increased importance of travel agents in airline distribution systems. In the United States today, for example, well over 70 percent of all airline tickets are written by travel agents.

As both passengers and airlines increased their reliance on travel agents to handle their reservations and ticketing requirements, an airline's ability to secure effective access to travel agencies became a critical competitive variable. To strengthen and expand their access to travel agencies, several airlines have developed computerized reservation systems (CRS), which automate many travel agency functions and reduce the agencies' unit costs for booking reservations and issuing tickets.

Led by United and American Airlines, U.S. airlines have introduced increasingly sophisticated computerized reservations systems. In order to maximize the benefits they obtain from their proprietary CRS services, each carrier initially built certain biases into the CRS intended to encourage agents to book passengers on that airline's flights. The principal form of bias was for the system to display the airline's own flights first on the computer screen. Since travel agencies try to minimize the amount of time spent on each transaction, having "first screen" display can provide substantial advantages for airlines with widely used CRS services.

The cost of developing such systems and the difficulty of persuading travel agents to switch systems appear to preclude the existence of a large number of CRS vendors. Thus, it is not surprising to find that all of the top six U.S. airlines own a major CRS (TWA and Northwest jointly own the Pars system) (see Table 2–16).

Major airlines have also used data generated by their CRS networks to develop sophisticated seat allocation capabilities. As a result, these carriers have introduced a host of capacity

Table 2–16. U.S. CRS Market Share.

System	*Airline*	*No. of Travel Agent Locations*	*Percent of Agent Locations*	*Airline Market Share of RPMs*
Sabre	American	10,600	39.3	13.8
Apollo	United	7,400	27.4	15.9
SystemOne	Texas Air	5,000	18.5	19.5
Pars	TWA/Northwest	3,700	13.7	18.4
Datas II	Delta	3,000	11.1	11.6
Total		29,700	110.0	79.2

Note: Agent locations data are from airline reports. The percentage figure is calculated from the known total of 27,000 agents. The overlap is because some agents have more than one system. RPM market share is for the first nine months of 1986. Pan Am, with 5.9 percent of RPMs, is co-hosted on Sabre.

Source: *Airline Business* (Sutton, Surrey, United Kingdom), March 1987, p. 19.

controlled fares, each subject to different conditions, and all tailored to generate traffic without diverting higher fare, on-demand traffic to the lower fare offerings. In addition, airlines used CRS to gain competitively valuable information regarding travel agency bookings on their own and competitors' flights. Such information can be used to develop marketing programs aimed at inducing travel agencies to book reservations on flights offered by the CRS vendor.

Complaints about competitive abuses by major CRS vendors have precipitated administrative rulemakings by the CAB and the U.S. Department of Transportation,[6] as well as a number of antitrust suits against major CRS vendors.[7]

Frequent Flier Programs

Frequent traveler programs have proven to be extremely effective marketing tools in the deregulated U.S. air services market. These programs seek to develop "brand loyalty" among airline passengers by rewarding travelers with bonuses based on mileage flown and fare paid. Since the bonuses accrue as nontaxable income to the individual traveler (not to the employer who paid for the ticket), these programs also reduce the business traveler's incentive to fly with other carriers, even if they are less expensive.

The more extensive a carrier's route system, the easier it is for travelers to earn bonuses. In addition, the attractiveness of free flights increases as the number of destinations in the program increases. Thus, frequent traveler programs are particularly advantageous to larger airlines that serve extensive route systems and offer numerous destinations. The success of such programs in attracting the patronage of high-frequency travelers fuels further expansion of services via existing and new hubs.[8]

The Overall Impact of Deregulation on Passenger Airlines

The U.S. airline industry structure that has emerged from a decade of deregulated competition is characterized by the development of a relatively small number (fewer than ten) of truly national, increasingly international *single-carrier air transportation networks*. These multi-hub networks appear to produce the type of large economies of scale and scope characteristic of multiproduct firms.[9] To expand their networks, major airlines are extending their control, acquisition or code-sharing agreements, to include the small aircraft operations that provide service to their hubs.[10] The importance of the network system to a deregulated airline industry has significant implications for efforts to liberalize trade in air services. These implications will be explored in Chapter 6.

By mid-1987, the heightened competition spawned by deregulation and a hands-off approach to airline mergers by the Reagan administration's Department of Transportation had resulted in significant structural changes and increased concentration in the U.S. airline industry. Through acquisition and internal growth, fewer than ten U.S. mega-carriers, each with national—and increasingly international—route networks emanating from its domestic hubs, have come to dominate the U.S. airline industry. The market share of the five largest U.S. airlines increased from 63.5 percent in 1978 to 71.7 percent by 1987.[11] Table 2–17 shows the consolidation that occurred between 1985 and 1987.

The Impact of Deregulation on the U.S. Air Cargo Industry

Deregulation has also produced substantial changes in the U.S. air cargo industry. Heightened competition between and within the deregulated U.S. trucking, airline, and air cargo industries has forced several major U.S. airlines to discontinue

Table 2–17. U.S. Airline Market Share in RPMs (percent).

	1985		8 Months 1987
1. American	13.1	1. Texas Air	19.038
2. United	12.4	2. United	16.852
3. Eastern	9.9	3. American	13.891
4. TWA	9.5	4. Delta	11.524
5. Delta	9.0	5. Northwest	10.383
6. Pan American	8.1	6. TWA	8.376
7. Northwest	6.7	7. Pan American	6.488
8. Continental	4.9	8. USAir/PSA/Piedmont	7.088
9. People Express	3.3	9. Southwest	1.365
10. Republic	3.2	10. America West	1.365
11. Western	3.1	Total	96.617
12. USAir	2.9		
13. Piedmont	2.4		
14. Southwest	1.6		
Total	90.1		

Sources: Air Transport Association Annual Reports (Washington, D.C., 1985); *Aviation Daily*, September 29, 1987.

freighter operations in the U.S. domestic market and forced Flying Tigers, the largest all-cargo airline, into a major retrenchment.

Deregulation also permitted the development and rapid expansion of the small-package air express industry. Figures 2–4 and 2–5 show the growth of express-package volumes and revenues experienced by the Federal Express Corporation, the firm that pioneered the development of the small-package express business. Federal Express is the largest air express company, with a market share estimated at between 50 and 60 percent of the U.S. small-package express market.

Over the past decade, Federal Express has eclipsed Flying Tigers as the largest U.S. cargo airline in both total domestic air freight tonnage and air freight revenues. Federal now ranks second behind Tigers among U.S. airlines in total (domestic and international) tonnage and third behind Tigers and Northwest in total RTKs (see Table 2–11). United Parcel Service (UPS), another rapidly growing provider of next-day parcel delivery, has recently

Figure 2–4. Federal Express Corporation Twelve-Year Package-Volume History.

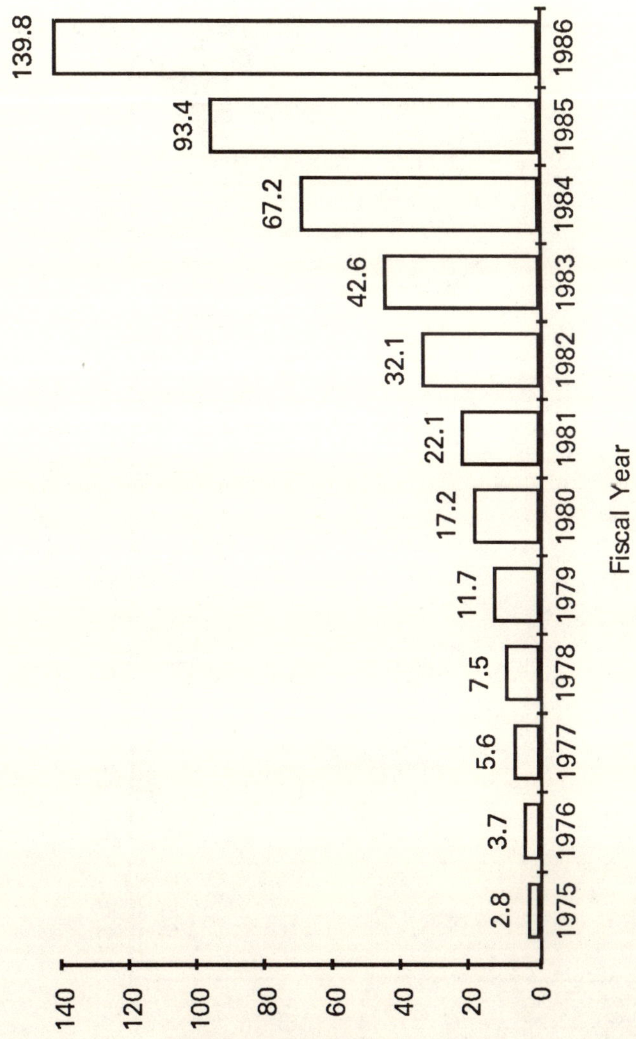

Source: Federal Express Corporation, annual reports.

Figure 2–5. Federal Express Corporation Twelve-Year Revenue History.

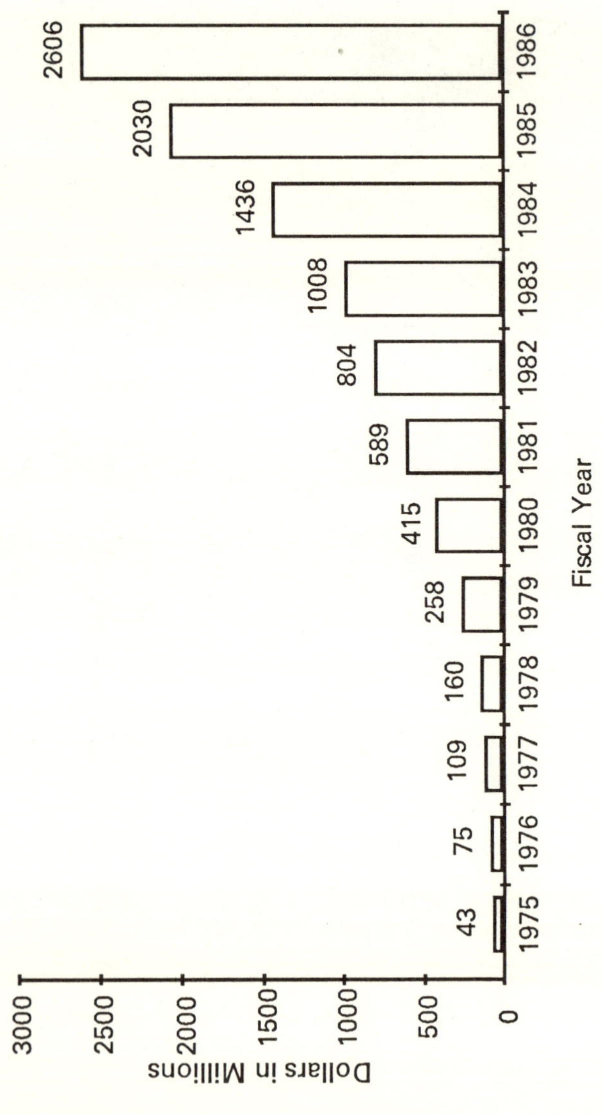

Source: Federal Express Corporation, annual reports.

announced its intention to operate its own cargo airline. With its strong position in the surface and air small-package markets, a substantial position in the air cargo market, a growing position in international markets, and a large fleet of modern aircraft, UPS is likely to join Federal Express in the top rank of U.S. and world cargo airlines.

THE INTERNATIONAL IMPLICATIONS OF U.S. DEREGULATION

The restructuring of the U.S. airline industry has had important international consequences. Overall, it has strengthened U.S. airlines' competitiveness vis-à-vis foreign airlines, particularly for international traffic to and from the United States. It has also increased competition among U.S. airlines for international traffic and reduced the number of U.S. airlines feeding traffic to foreign airlines at their U.S. gateways. Using the traffic leverage inherent in their large domestic hubs, U.S. airlines have aggressively expanded their networks to include new international markets.

Foreign airlines are thus facing competitive pressure in international markets from larger and increasingly efficient U.S. airlines. Plagued by small domestic markets, restrictive international agreements, and often-inefficient airlines, national governments are beginning to accept market-opening measures in their own domestic and international markets. These governments increasingly view liberalization as either inevitable or essential to maintain the viability of their airlines in an increasingly competitive marketplace.

Meanwhile, foreign airlines are not relying solely on their governments to cope with the effects of deregulation. European carriers are scrambling to find ways to offset the advantages enjoyed by large U.S. carriers. Merging is one approach. The chairman of British Caledonian Airways, for example, cited the strength of U.S. mega-carriers as a primary reason behind the merger of British Caledonian with British Airways (BA). BA has also negotiated a code-sharing agreement with United in an effort to expand its access to interior U.S. traffic.

In addition, SAS and Sabena have conducted extensive negotiations to merge their airline operations, while the chairman of Alitalia openly discusses his desire to acquire or merge with another European carrier in order to match the U.S. carrier strengths. Two consortia of European airlines cited similar reasons for the mid-1987 establishment of their own computerized reservations systems. In the Pacific Basin, too, carriers have expressed like concerns in recent years as U.S. mega-carriers, including Delta, United, American, and Continental, entered Pacific Basin markets in force.

Foreign governments have also begun to press the United States to open its domestic market. Canada, for example, proposed an exchange of rights that would permit each nation's airlines to carry domestic traffic in the other's territory. Some European airlines are suggesting that the rights of U.S. airlines to carry traffic within Europe should be eliminated if the U.S. market is not opened to European airlines, while Britain's transport minister has publicly indicated the United Kingdom's desire to permit British airlines to own U.S. airlines and vice versa.

NOTES

1. International Air Transport Association, *World Air Transport Statistics, 1986* (Montreal:IATA, 1987), p. 7.
2. "Small Is Beautiful," *Airline Business*, October 1987, p. 18.
3. Readers interested in a more detailed description of CAB regulation of the airline industry should see Elizabeth Bailey, Daniel Kaplan, and David Graham, *Deregulating the Airlines* (Cambridge, Mass.: MIT Press, 1985). See also Staff Report, *Regulatory Reform at the CAB* (Washington, D.C.: U.S. Civil Aeronautics Board, 1975). For an earlier treatment, see L.S. Keyes, *Federal Control of Entry into Air Transportation* (Cambridge, Mass.: Harvard University Press, 1949).
4. Public Law No. 95-504, 92 Stat. 1705 (codified as amended in various sections of 49 U.S.C.).

5. For a more detailed examination of the impact of deregulation, see Bailey et al., *Deregulating the Airlines*; Michael Levine, "Airline Competition in Deregulated Markets: Theory, Firm Strategy and Public Policy," *Yale Journal on Regulation* 4 (April 1987): 393–494; M. Brenner, J. Leet, and E. Schott, *Airline Deregulation* (Eno Foundation, 1985).
6. 49 Federal Register 32,540 (1984); 14 C.F.R. Section 255.6 (1986).
7. In re Air Passenger Computer Reservation Systems Antitrust Litigation, MDL-667 (C.D. Cal consolidated January 31, 1986).
8. Levine, "Airline Competition."
9. Ibid.; also E. Bailey and A. Freidlander, "Market Structure and Multiproduct Industries," *Journal of Economic Literature* 20 (September 1982): 1024.
10. Code-sharing is the practice of listing on CRS displays a flight of one airline under two or more codes, its own (for example, UA is United) and that of another carrier (for example, British Airways).
11. *Airline Economics* ranked the top five in 1978 as United, American, Eastern, TWA, and Delta; the top five in 1987 were Texas Air, United, American, Delta, and Northwest.

3

THE LEGAL AND INSTITUTIONAL REGIME GOVERNING INTERNATIONAL AIR SERVICES

International air services are governed today by legal and institutional arrangements developed during the late 1940s. Like the GATT regime that governs international trade in goods, the international regime for air services arose from the failure of nations to agree on a more comprehensive, multilateral system. As a result, air services in the postwar period have developed under a hodge-podge of multilateral and bilateral agreements involving governments and airlines.[1]

Multilateral agreements among governments generally cover international legal matters that affect the operation of civil aircraft, such as overflight rights, nationality of aircraft, and minimum safety, maintenance, and training standards. Bilateral agreements deal principally, but not exclusively, with the exchange of substantive economic rights. Bilaterals also cover certain technical safety and security issues as well as ancillary rights essential to the enjoyment of the economic rights granted in the agreement. These include such matters as currency conversion, profit repatriation, and mutual recognition of licenses.

Multilateral agreements among airlines cover an array of technical and facilitation matters, trade association activities, and pricing agreements. Airlines sometimes enter bilateral agreements with other carriers addressing such matters as division of capacity or traffic, pricing, reciprocal access to reservations systems, maintenance, ground handling, and joint operations. Table 3–1 summarizes the types of multilateral and bilateral agreements that govern international air services.

Table 3–1. An Overview of International Aviation Agreements.

Multilateral	*Bilateral*
	Intergovernmental
Chicago Convention	Air Service Agreements
International Civil Aviation Organization	Economic rights
Constitution	Entry
Technical and safety standards	Routes and traffic
Technical and safety assistance	Capacity
	Pricing
Framework regulations	Ancillary rights
Sovereignty over airspace	Commercial operations
Nationality of aircraft	Currency conversion
	Licensing
	Profit repatriation, etc.
International Air Services Transit Agreement (IASTA)	
Transit rights	
Technical stops	
	Intercarrier
International Air Transport Association (IATA)	Airline-to-Airline
Tariff conferences	Pooling
Negotiate prices, terms, conditions	Traffic
Passenger and cargo	Revenues
Facilitation agreements	Capacity limitation
Interline connections	Prices
Travel agent accreditation	Levels
Financial clearinghouse	Conditions
Other matters	
Trade association activities	Marketing
Educate/lobby governments	CRS
Coordinate industry positions	Joint fares, etc.
	Operations
	Aircraft handling
	Maintenance
	Passenger services
	Other services

MULTILATERAL AIR SERVICES AGREEMENTS

The Chicago Conference

In 1944 the Chicago Conference on International Civil Aviation was convened to develop an acceptable framework for governing postwar civil aviation. The Chicago Conference was the air services counterpart to the Havana Conference for trade in goods, and its aim was to develop a framework to keep the newly emerging air services industry from becoming mired in mercantilistic national policies.

The Conference ultimately developed several agreements for ratification, including the Chicago Convention on International Aviation. The Convention contains the constitution for the International Civil Aviation Organization (ICAO), which is described below. It also establishes certain legal principles that apply to civil aviation between and among signatories. For example, it confirms a nation's sovereignty over the airspace above its territory and establishes rules governing the nationality of aircraft.

The Chicago Conference also produced the International Air Services Transit Agreement (IASTA), by which scheduled airlines of signatory countries are permitted to transit the airspace of other signatories and to make technical (nontraffic) stops in the territories of signatory states. Perhaps because of its similarity to traditional maritime doctrines of navigational freedom and the right to enter foreign ports for nontraffic purposes, IASTA has been ratified by more than 100 nations.

Less successful was the Conference's effort to negotiate a liberal exchange of route rights on a multilateral basis. The drafters of the so-called Five Freedoms Agreement envisioned it as the keystone of a new, multilateral regime for the governance of air services. Opposition was widespread, however, led by the United Kingdom and joined by virtually every country with a significant amount of air traffic. These nations were unwilling to grant access to the airlines of a nation without taking into consideration the amount of traffic that nation generated. In addition, opponents feared that airlines from the United States would dominate world markets in a liberal air services system. Among the world's major powers, only the United States continued to press for a liberal, multilateral regime. Eventually, however, the strong opposition of Pan American Airways led the United States to withdraw its support, and the agreement was never ratified.[2]

The International Civil Aviation Organization (ICAO)

Despite the Chicago conferees' inability to negotiate a ratifiable multilateral regime for the exchange of economic rights, the Conference did create an international body to address international aviation matters—the International Civil Aviation Organization, or ICAO. The lack of agreement on economic rights restricted ICAO's focus to technical and safety matters.

Over the past four decades, ICAO has worked with national regulatory authorities, such as the U.S. Federal Aviation Administration and the U.K. Civil Aviation Authority, to develop safety and other technical aviation standards and to recommend their adoption by member states. ICAO has also helped developing countries to bring their technical, safety, and operational standards in line with world standards.

Like many international bodies during the 1970s, ICAO's General Assembly became increasingly politicized, particularly as a forum for third world complaints against the developed nations. ICAO's attempts to play a more active role in the economic aspects of civil air services have had a distinctly protectionist bent, which at one point made the United States consider withdrawing from the organization. ICAO also became a natural and convenient forum for opponents of the U.S. competitive international policy in the early 1980s.

The International Air Transport Association (IATA)

The failure of nations to ratify the International Air Transport Agreement left international aviation without a general set of rules governing either the exchange of economic rights or the restrictions that governments might impose on airline operations. The International Air Transport Association soon stepped in to fill the void. In the absence of a governmentally agreed-upon charter for international air services, IATA substituted agreements among airlines. It became an overseas representative to the growing number of world airlines and, through member airlines, a vehicle for minimizing government restrictions on international airline operations. By establishing agreements governing pricing and such other matters as interline connections, travel agent accreditation, and clearinghouse procedures for settling ticket revenue balances among members, and through a range of trade association activities covering airports, maintenance, training, and safety, IATA thus played a threefold role as

- a cartel for airlines to agree upon prices,
- an international airline trade association, and
- a surrogate for a multilateral governmental agreement.

It is interesting to note that Switzerland regards IATA as an international organization and exempts its employees' salaries from taxation. IATA has functioned prominently as a government surrogate in the case of developing countries and other nations without aviation expertise independent of the national airline. Elsewhere, as in the United States and the United Kingdom, for example, national governments possess considerable independent aviation expertise, so IATA has played a less prominent role in their aviation affairs.

For thirty years, however, even the United States routinely approved the jointly agreed-upon airline fares submitted by IATA carriers. Not until the United States embarked on deregulation in earnest did it review IATA's price-setting and other activities. Not surprisingly, delegating rate-making authority to an airline cartel had led to a fare structure that was high enough to protect less-efficient airlines and generally lacking in low fares. Eventually, competition from charter flights and from Laker Airways prompted scheduled airlines to introduce the Super Apex (discount) fare and ultimately led to the collapse of IATA rate-making on the North Atlantic. IATA's role in the development and evolution of the U.S. competitive aviation policy is discussed in Chapter 5.

BILATERAL AIR SERVICE AGREEMENTS

Bilateral air service agreements today govern both access to and competition within international air service routes. These agreements define the exchange of economic rights including entry, capacity, routes, and pricing as well as important ancillary rights in commercial operations and administrative procedures.[3]

Economic Rights

The substantive economic rights negotiated in bilateral air service agreements can be grouped into four categories for international air services: entry and designation, capacity, route and traffic rights, and pricing. The ability of a government to restrict access and competition on international routes by setting strict bilateral limits on these economic rights constitutes the most obvious barrier to liberalized air services trade.

Entry and Designation. Airlines are not free to enter international markets of their own choosing. To serve an international route, an airline must first be designated by its government to provide scheduled service on that route. That government's right to designate an airline comes from an agreement with the country at the other end of the route. Thus, the U.S. right to designate carriers to serve the United Kingdom is established by the

U.S.-U.K. Air Services Agreement. In current practice, bilateral agreements establish a range of rights from a strict limit of one carrier per country through an unrestricted number of carriers.

Except for their agreements with the United States, most nations have, until recently, accepted only a single designated carrier per party. Virtually every U.S. air service agreement permits some form of multiple designation. The Bermuda I standard form air service agreement, on which the majority of existing air service agreements are based, permits a party to designate "an airline or airlines"[4] on the route(s) established by the agreement. This language allows each party to make multiple carrier designations. The United States has interpreted this language as permitting each party to designate as many carriers as it chooses. Since 1978 U.S. air service agreements have included language explicitly establishing unlimited designation rights.

Entry and access restrictions also apply to nonscheduled and charter operators for both passenger and cargo air services. Charters played an important competitive role in the North Atlantic market as a low-fare, competitive threat to the scheduled service cartel beginning in the early 1970s. With the breakdown of IATA rate agreements and the introduction of low-fare scheduled services, however, charters' competitive role on the North Atlantic has diminished (see Table 2–11).

Charters remain a major factor in intra-European markets, where they have traditionally carried most of the holiday traffic, particularly to "sun spots" such as the Costa del Sol and Greece. As the European Community moves toward its 1992 target for a more open internal market in air services, however, many experts believe that charters will lose market share to scheduled airlines given new competitive freedom to enter traditional charter markets.

In the many cases where charter rights are not covered under bilateral agreements, governments have virtually unlimited discretion in dealing with these operations. Countries that permit international charter operations often limit them to prevent competition with scheduled service carriers or impose constraints (such as uplift ratios or package purchase requirements) aimed at preventing the diversion of traffic from scheduled carriers to charters.

Since 1978 the United States has sought (with only modest success) substantial liberalization of existing bilateral charter air services. The U.S.-Belgium agreement, for example, permits charter carriers unlimited access, applies the least restrictive national charter rules, and effectively puts charter carriers on equal competitive footing with scheduled carriers.

The differences between the U.S. and other nations' attitudes toward liberalized entry policies reflect in part the basic differences in scale between the large U.S. domestic market and numerous airlines and the small domestic markets and single national carriers typical of other countries. But they also reflect the strong mercantilistic tendencies characteristic of most nations' approaches to international air services.

Capacity. The amount of capacity that a carrier may provide on an international route also falls under the purview of bilateral agreements. Most U.S. agreements contain Bermuda I capacity principles that permit each carrier to determine its own capacity subject to ex post facto review at the option of either government.[5] A few recent U.S. bilaterals contain language that further strengthens the right of each carrier to determine its own capacity without governmental interference.

In agreements to which the United States is not party, however, carrier capacity is typically established between governments and/or airlines, a practice known as predetermination. By limiting the amount of capacity available on a route and dividing it between each nation's airlines, such bilaterals severely restrict the potential for competition.

Recently, predetermination of capacity on routes within the European Common Market has come under scrutiny. The European Court has ruled that the Treaty of Rome applies to air services,[6] while the EC Commission has indicated that restrictions such as predetermination violate the Treaty of Rome's competition articles and existing Community regulations. Member states were able to agree on new EC air services rules when the Commission threatened to initiate enforcement action.

Controls over the capacity offered on passenger services also constrain the amount of available cargo capacity by reducing the amount of bellyhold capacity on the route. Since cargo service is directly linked to the productive sector—and to politically powerful interests—in most economies, however, air cargo capacity is less commonly restricted.

Route and Traffic Rights. A route describes the points (cities) served (such as the New York–London–Frankfurt route) by a designated airline. Traffic rights establish the type of traffic that designated airlines are permitted to carry over that route. Third- and Fourth-Freedom traffic rights (established by the Chicago Convention) allow a designated airline to carry traffic between its home country and the territory of the other bilateral partner. That is, traffic between the United States and Great Britain may be carried by an airline designated to serve the New York–London route. Sometimes additional traffic rights, called Fifth-Freedom traffic rights, are negotiated to permit the carriage of traffic between the territory of the other party and a third country. Pan American's right to carry local traffic from London to Frankfurt (on its New York–London–Frankfurt flight) illustrates a Fifth-Freedom right. International traffic that originates behind a carrier's homeland (for instance, South American traffic flying to Europe via New York on Pan American) is known as Sixth-Freedom traffic. There is a longstanding legal argument as to whether Sixth-Freedom traffic is subject to bilateral regulation.[7] As a practical matter, such traffic is extremely difficult to control without the consent of the Sixth-Freedom carrier (or its government) since it involves a combination of two streams of Third- and Fourth-Freedom traffic (such as Brazil–New York and New York–London). Chapter 6 describes the effect of a nation's location on the ability of its airlines to use Sixth-Freedom traffic flows to expand its share of international trade in air services.

As discussed in Chapter 2, having access to such behind or beyond the gateway traffic may be crucial to the viability of international air services. But the right to compete in foreign international (Fifth-Freedom) markets is typically restricted and often subject to strict limitations. Thus, except for the carriage of Sixth-Freedom traffic, the possibility for trade is often effectively limited to routes touching a carrier's home country where it is often further constrained by capacity predetermination and government price regulation. Under such circumstances, *net* trade in air services is significantly restricted.

The emergence of air service networks for both passenger and cargo services has further underscored the competitive importance of having access to numerous routes. The more extensive an airline's route structure, the greater number of destinations and service options it can offer to passengers and shippers, thus the more valuable the network is to both airlines and their customers.

Pricing. A variety of bilateral provisions governs the pricing of international air services. The most liberal system is double disapproval, under which a carrier's proposed fare can be rejected only if both governments disapprove the proposed price. This is the pricing article that the United States favors as part of its "model" procompetitive bilateral. Belgium, Israel, the Netherlands, and Korea, among others, have signed agreements with double disapproval pricing. The more standard and restrictive Bermuda I pricing provision is the double approval article, which permits either party to veto unilaterally any price for transport to or from its territory.

Between these extremes lie a number of other systems. Somewhat more restrictive than double disapproval is country-of-origin pricing, which gives each party the right to disapprove only those tariffs applicable to traffic originating in its own territory. Until it was revised in 1987, the U.S.-Netherlands agreement permitted the Dutch to disapprove tariffs for traffic originating in the Netherlands, and the United States similar disapproval rights for traffic originating within its borders.[8] The home-state approval system makes an airline's prices subject to control only by its national government, thereby precluding intervention by foreign governments.

A double-disapproval zone system permits a fare falling within agreed-upon zones to become effective unless both governments disapprove it. For fares outside of the zones, either a country-of-origin or a double-approval regime applies. The U.S. agreement with the Philippines contains a double-disapproval zone pricing article. Such a system has also been negotiated multilaterally between the U.S. and the member states of the European Civil Aviation Conference (ECAC). Under the provisions of that agreement, each signatory applies either the U.S.-ECAC zones or the pricing regime in its bilateral with the United States, whichever is more liberal.

Although cargo is nominally subject to the same pricing system as are passenger services, air cargo pricing in most major markets has been substantially deregulated. A number of factors have contributed to this outcome, including

- the small number and sophistication of international air cargo shippers, principally freight forwarders and large corporations;
- the availability of ample bellyhold cargo capacity, a by-product of using wide-body aircraft for passenger air services;
- the insensitivity of many shippers to routing circuity, thereby increasing the number of airlines and routings competing for cargo;
- the vast array of cargo tariffs permitting invisible price reductions based on the characterization of cargo to meet lower tariff requirements; and
- the ability of deregulated trucking firms to carry air cargo to competing airlines at alternative gateways, particularly in the large European and North American markets.

Ancillary Rights

Bilateral air service agreements also govern ancillary rights, which can be critical to achieving competitiveness in international air services markets. Bilaterals typically contain provisions for local currency conversions, profit repatriation, access to local distribution channels (such as travel agents and computerized reservations systems), ground handling, airport and airways user charges, and administrative matters such as mutual recognition of licenses, aviation safety and security, operating permits, compliance with local laws, and customs duties. Somewhat less successfully, current agreements cover issues involving government-owned monopolies, domestic regulatory policies, and market structure in domestic markets.

As in other services industries, ancillary factors in air services can raise troublesome barriers for service firms seeking to serve foreign markets. Chapter 4 discusses examples of problems involving airport user charges, computer reservations systems, and domestic market structure.

THE DUTCH PLURILATERAL

Another attempt to develop a multilateral regime governing economic rights in air services was initiated in 1980 by a Dutch proposal for a "plurilateral" agreement. As formulated, the Dutch plurilateral envisioned a type of super-GATT for air services. It proposed selective liberalization of air services (that is, only between or among parties prepared to accept significant liberalization) but allowed for selective protectionism between parties; it maintained the status quo in respect to nonsignatory third countries. The Dutch proposal also contemplated "market access on a nondiscriminatory and MFN basis."[9] Despite vigorous Dutch promotion efforts, the plurilateral concept was not given serious consideration by other countries.

The lack of interest in the Dutch proposal was due to the fact that Holland is a small nation with a large, efficient, and very competitive airline. Thus, the major traffic-generating countries in Europe, particularly Germany and France, have traditionally opposed Dutch efforts to open their markets. Similarly, U.S. airlines have often opposed expansion of Dutch traffic rights and are not readily accepting the plurilateral proposal.

Despite the initial lack of support for the Dutch plurilateral proposal, further liberalization of trade in air services will most likely require a less-than-universal (no unconditional MFN) multilateral air services agreement conceptually similar to that proposed by the Dutch. Such an approach is discussed in Chapter 7.

NOTES

1. For a comprehensive treatment see B. Cheng, *The Law of International Air Transport* (London: Stevens, 1962).
2. W. Pogue, "International Civil Air Transport Transition Following WWII," MIT Flight Transportation Laboratory, Report FTL-R79-6, June 1979.
3. "Provisions in U.S. International Air Transport Agreements," Air Transport Association of America, Washington, D.C., 1985.
4. Ibid., p. 346.
5. Several U.S. bilateral partners take the position that Bermuda I language permits a government to limit capacity prospectively.
6. *Nouvelles Frontieres* (Ministere Public vs. Lucas Asjes and Others), European Court of Justice, April 1986.
7. H.A. Wassenbergh, "Reflections on the Sixth Freedom Question," in H.A. Wassenbergh and H.P. van Fenema, eds., *International Air Transportation for the Eighties* (Deventer, the Netherlands: Kluwer Publishers 1981), p. 189.
8. 1978 Protocol to the 1957 Air Services Agreement between the Kingdom of the Netherlands and the United States of America, T.I.A.S. 8998.
9. "International Air Transport, A Trade in Services," H.A. Wassenbergh, undated manuscript. See also K. Veenstra, "The 'Plurilateral Air Transport Agreement': A Draft for a Better Regulatory Instrument," in H.A. Wassenbergh and H.P. van Fenema, *International Air Transportation for the Eighties*, pp. 215 ff.

4

BARRIERS TO LIBERALIZATION OF TRADE IN AIR SERVICES

The barriers to liberalized trade in air services can be grouped into four categories: (1) bilateral restrictions that prevent entry or directly restrict the competitiveness of foreign airlines, (2) domestic regulatory systems, (3) conditions and restrictions in ancillary domestic markets that impair a foreign carrier's ability to compete and (4) government ownership and subsidization of airlines.[1]

BILATERAL RESTRICTIONS

Entry

Initial market access in air services is defined and limited by the scope of a carrier's route rights and the type and quantity of traffic it may carry over those routes: without the consent of a sovereign state, an airline enjoys no general right to pick up or set down passengers or cargo in its territory. Hence, the first, and in many cases most formidable, barrier to liberalization of trade in air services is the requirement to negotiate entry, capacity, and the types of traffic that can be carried. Countries that generate a large amount of traffic have strong incentives to protect their traffic from the "have not" countries in order to trade it to other "haves" for access to their larger traffic bases.

The traditional approach to bargaining in air service negotiations has been to barter access to one nation's traffic in exchange for access to the other country's traffic. To compensate for the fact that one nation's traffic pool may be significantly larger, or to offset existing market access barriers in the second country (see discussion below), the latter's access may be limited in terms of the number of carriers permitted, gateways served, type of traffic allowed, prices charged, or capacity offered.

Routes

Bilaterally imposed restrictions on the routes served by international airlines effectively define airlines' markets and can severely restrict their competitiveness. Agreements typically permit an airline to carry traffic from its home country to specified gateways in the foreign country. Small countries, such as Holland or Belgium, can be effectively served through a single gateway, but multiple gateways may be required for larger countries with more dispersed population concentrations (such as Australia, Brazil, Canada, India, Japan, and the United States). Thus, bilaterally defined routes and gateways afford some international airlines superior market access to that of their competitors.

Gaining access to purely domestic traffic as well as international routes behind the homeland can also enhance a carrier's international competitiveness. The reason is simple: the incremental traffic support provided by domestic (and international) services behind the gateway is often essential to sustain competitive service on long-haul international routes. Deprived of the right to enter foreign domestic and international markets and the right to establish an airline in a foreign jurisdiction, efficient airlines are less likely to realize economies of scale and scope and to otherwise capitalize on their comparative strengths in world air services markets. Thus, the barriers posed by restrictions on access to international routes are compounded by the complete denial of access to domestic air service markets.

The rapid development of hub-and-spoke operations by U.S. (and some foreign) airlines has highlighted this aspect of the market access problem. Carriers such as TWA, Pan American, Continental, American, Delta, and Northwest, for example, now offer connecting services from their U.S. gateways to hundreds of domestic points and to numerous international destinations as well. Since hub locations are generally restricted to a carrier's home territory, geography confers certain natural advantages. Carriers with hubs farthest west in Europe (British Airways at London and KLM in Holland) have a significant advantage over internal European competitors for providing service across the North Atlantic, since they can combine traffic flows over their hubs with less circuity and delay than carriers with interior gateways. Hence, it is more efficient for British Airways to serve the France-U.S. market than for Air France to serve the U.K.-U.S. market.

Pricing

Governmental restrictions on the pricing of international air services can also severely restrict market access. Switzerland's refusal to approve People Express' low fares, for example, prevented that carrier from entering the market. Since People Express' strategy depended on offering low fares for its no-frills, high-density service, the Swiss action forced the carrier to abandon either its strategy or the U.S.-Switzerland market. It chose the latter.

Governments also use their power to disapprove prices to prevent the introduction of new "products," such as business-class or charter-class services, that they believe would harm their national carriers. The Venezuelan government, for instance, refused to permit Pan American to offer business-class fares in the Venezuela-U.S. market because the local flag carrier, Viasa, was unwilling to offer such service. (Viasa apparently lacked a computer system capable of managing a multiclass seat inventory.) Similarly, the Scandinavian governments waged a determined effort to prevent Northwest Airlines from offering first-class accommodations to business-class passengers, Northwest's competitive response to SAS's renowned first-class service. Numerous governments—including those of the United States in the case of Freddie Laker and the United Kingdom for People Express—have used their control over airline prices to prevent or delay the introduction of low-priced, no-frills air services.

Capacity

Another primary access barrier is governmental insistence that air service agreements explicitly limit the amount of capacity on airlines serving their territories. Several U.S. agreements with protectionistic South American countries, for example, limit the carriers of each party to a specified number of flights and sometimes include a formula for determining aircraft equivalencies (such as one DC-10 frequency = two B-727 frequencies). Agreements that do not involve the United States are generally even more restrictive. Many contain pooling arrangements, by which the traffic (or revenue) is divided between the limited number of airlines permitted to serve the market.

In combination with the economies of large aircraft operations, bilateral restrictions that limit access to domestic and international traffic can significantly impair the competitiveness of otherwise efficient airlines. Carriers with access to large domestic and/or international markets thus enjoy a distinct advantage under a bilateral regime.

In sum, restrictions on entry, capacity, traffic, and pricing imposed by bilateral air service agreement and buttressed by domestic legal restrictions on the right of establishment, are major obstacles in the path of negotiators seeking to liberalize trade in air services. The reliance upon bilateral agreements in conjunction with the doctrine of national sovereignty over territorial airspace encourages nations to approach air service negotiations mercantilistically, trading access to each other's traffic in rough proportion to the amount of traffic available.

DOMESTIC REGULATORY POLICIES

Lacking the right to enter foreign domestic markets and to establish an airline in a foreign jurisdiction, otherwise efficient airlines may be unable to attain sufficient economies of scale and scope to compete successfully in world air services markets. Thus, regulatory policies that exclude foreign airlines from domestic markets or restrict their ability to compete effectively in those markets constitute a substantial barrier to liberalized trade in air services.

Having effective access to local and domestic traffic is becoming increasingly important to support economically viable services in international markets. The incremental international traffic support provided by domestic services behind a carrier's gateway often makes the difference between profit and loss on long-haul international routes. But without the right to carry domestic traffic on such behind-gateway routes, foreign airlines cannot serve those routes economically.

Foreign airlines serving the United States traditionally depended upon numerous U.S. domestic airlines to serve traffic destined (or originating) behind their U.S. gateways. That is, Air France (AF) relied on United to get traffic from Cleveland to the AF gateway at New York. Since deregulation, however, this source of traffic support is less reliable due to international expansion by former U.S. domestic carriers, domestic expansion by U.S. international airlines, and a reduction in the number of U.S. commercial airlines. TWA, Pan American, Continental, American, Delta, Northwest, and Piedmont/USAir now offer single-carrier service to Europe from hundreds of cities in the United States.

The problem is often worse in domestic markets outside the United States where airline service has traditionally been provided by a single monopoly carrier, often owned in whole or in part by the state. When the domestic monopoly airline is also the international flag carrier, as in the case of West Germany, for example, foreign airlines must rely on their major competitor for access to nongateway traffic in the foreign market. In other cases, such as France, the domestic monopolies are held by other carriers. In both cases, however, the national flag carrier enjoys an advantage over foreign competitors in accessing nongateway traffic in its home market.

RESTRICTIONS IN ANCILLARY MARKETS

Regulation of competition and market structure in related industries can also impair the competitiveness of foreign airlines in international air services. Government-owned or -protected monopolies that provide airport facilities, ground handling (and other airport) services, and distribution (that is, reservation and ticketing services, as well as cargo pickup and delivery) services have all spawned intergovernmental disputes in recent years.

Distribution Systems

Computerized Travel Agent Reservations Systems. Computerized reservations systems have spurred contentious market-access issues around the globe. Travel agents today write a very large proportion of all scheduled airline tickets—more than 70 percent of the tickets issued in the United States. The proliferation of fares and rapid changes in fares and schedules have made instantaneous access to fares, schedules, and seat inventories critical in the airlines' competition for the patronage and loyalty of travel agents. Since the less time a travel agency spends on each transaction, the more transactions and commissions that agency can generate, each airline customer reservation system (CRS) is typically designed to display its own flights first on the computer screen, thereby giving the carrier an edge over its competitors.

Further, an airline with many flights to and from a particular city can also offer more attractive and cost-effective incentive programs to encourage travel agencies to use its CRS. The relatively minor market presence of foreign carriers in most national markets combined with the substantial capital investments required to establish a new CRS initially discouraged carriers from introducing their own systems into foreign markets. More recently, however, U.S. carriers have begun to market their CRS products abroad, where they have encountered stiff resistance and lack of cooperation by local carriers, particularly in Europe.

Control of Traffic through Agents or Forwarders. Flying Tigers, the U.S. all-cargo airline, has complained that the ownership of Nippon All-Cargo Airlines by a group of major Japanese freight forwarders has put Tigers at an unfair disadvantage in seeking access to the Japanese cargo market. Since Japanese forwarders effectively control the movement of air cargo to and from the airports in Japan, according to Tigers they are able to shift business away from Flying Tigers. Yet Japanese restrictions on foreign ownership of forwarders prevent Tigers from effecting a counter vertical integration strategy.

A similar problem may emerge in passenger markets where the national flag airline, such as SAS in Scandinavia, acquires dominant tour wholesalers and travel agencies. Another problem involves the refusal of British Airways to authorize American Airlines to issue BA tickets on American's Sabre System, a competing CRS. Since BA is the largest U.K. carrier, its refusal has blocked Sabre's access to British travel agents who must be able to issue BA tickets.

U.S. small-package express carriers, such as Federal Express and UPS, have encountered substantial distribution problems created by national postal authorities (for example, the German Bundespost) that have impeded U.S. carrier efforts to establish local distribution systems because such services involve the carriage of materials over which the postal authorities have a statutory monopoly. (Federal Express initially encountered the same objections from the U.S. Postal Service, which relented when Federal offered to pay postage for the documents that Federal delivered.)

Traffic reservation schemes, such as "fly American" requirements for U.S. government travelers, cabotage, restrictions, and cargo preference requirements, also restrict market access for international cargo and passenger airlines.

Airport/Airways Issues

Facilities. Discrimination in granting access to passenger or cargo terminals, customs clearance facilities, and fuel supplies has also given rise to numerous grievances by international airlines. Attaining access to adequate cargo terminal facilities, for example, became a significant point of contention between the United States and Korea when Korean Air built a major cargo facility on the U.S. West coast while preventing U.S. carriers from gaining access to such facilities in Korea.[2] Although such practices are more often found in developing countries, that is not always the case. The United States has raised the issue of discrimination with Germany regarding ground handling issues at Frankfurt and with the United Kingdom over a British decision that essentially denies access for all-cargo airlines at London's Heathrow Airport.

User Charges. Fees levied for airport facilities and related services have also been used to discriminate against foreign airlines and to impair the market for international air services. In one Latin American nation, excessive jet fuel prices charged to foreign airlines apparently subsidized the cost of fuel for that nation's flag carrier.[3]

A more sophisticated and troublesome version of the user charge problem is the system imposed by the British Airports Authority (BAA) at London airports.[4] The U.S. experience in attempting to change the BAA's system of apparently excessive and discriminatory user charges also illustrates the problems of ensuring that trade-in-services agreements are not undercut by other, unilaterally imposed measures.

The problem arose from the 1977 agreement between Britain and the International Monetary Fund, which imposed strict fiscal constraints on the British government. To meet these restrictions, the government imposed a tight cap on its public-sector borrowing requirement (PSBR). In a related measure designed to control capital commitments by state-owned enterprises, the British government established rate-of-return requirements that these enterprises had to meet in order to qualify for new investment funds.

Notwithstanding the obvious requirement for additional London airport capacity and the airport authority's existing airport-expansion program, HMG essentially denied the authority any PSBR allocation. Instead, as a "commercial enterprise," the authority was expected to recoup all its costs, including capital investment costs, directly and completely from current user fees. Conveniently ignored by the British government was the fact that long-term facilities such as airports are almost always financed by debt and amortized over an extended time period.

Caught between the heavy capital requirements of its major capacity-expansion program and the PSBR, and limited under the U.S.-U.K. bilateral agreement to imposing user charges that were "just and reasonable," the airport authority and the British government developed a creative solution. By adopting a current cost accounting system and rapidly revaluing assets upward to reflect high inflation rates, the BAA sought to justify much higher charges for users of London airports. To justify the additional charges needed to fund airport expansion entirely from current user fees, British government economists wove an elaborate theoretical argument based on the theory of long-run marginal costs.

The resulting huge user-fee increases, plus the questionable accounting and economic justifications rallied to defend the charges, raised a storm of protest and a lawsuit against the BAA by international airlines. They also raised serious questions as to whether the British actions were consistent with the U.S.-U.K. bilateral air services agreement.

In addition to its concern about the high fees, the U.S. government was particularly troubled by the fact that the peak prices coincided not with the peak level of airport (and British carrier) activities but with the times of transatlantic arrivals and departures. Since time zone differentials and popular arrival and departure times prevented transatlantic airlines from shifting operations to off-peak periods, and BAA restrictions prevented the carriers from shifting to less-congested terminal facilities, U.S. airlines serving London could not avoid or even mitigate the increased fees.

After extended and acrimonious consultations, an accommodation was reached by the British government, the United States, and the airlines entailing adjustments in BAA procedures that effectively froze U.S.-carrier user fees at London's Heathrow airport. In return, the U.S. airlines agreed to drop their lawsuit challenging the legality of the charges under British law. By 1987, however, airlines were again protesting the user-charge system at London's airports, raising the specter of further bilateral problems over this issue. The recent privatization of the British Airports Authority, which effectively turned a public monopolist into a private one, could complicate future negotiations if the British government continues to assert that its obligation is only to use best efforts and not to ensure reasonable fees.

Slots. Allocating access to take-off and landing slots may well become a major barrier to trade in international air services. Except in Japan, where the government has restricted access to Osaka because of airport noise and to Narita allegedly because of protests by adjacent farmers, airport access has not been a significant constraint. Since the U.S. air traffic controllers' strike in 1981, however, the prospect of increased access to New York–area airports and Chicago's O'Hare International Airport has been threatened by the inability of the airports and the surrounding air space to accommodate additional traffic safely. The U.S. Federal Aviation Administration has permitted slots to vest in their current operators and to become freely marketable among airlines and other parties able to pay the asking price. Under this standard, international carrier access to these restricted airports would be assured, at least for current operations.

Given the general population's heightened environmental awareness and sensitivity to aircraft noise in a number of major aviation powers, including Britain, the United States, and Japan, however, the prospects are increasing that airport access restrictions will become a more significant barrier in the future.

Labor Markets

In both the United States and Europe, organized labor has expressed concern about the potential impact of increased liberalization on domestic work forces. The fear is that liberalization might allow lower wage foreign airlines to take traffic and jobs away from their national airlines. In the United States the expansion of formerly domestic-only airlines into international markets has created a split within organized labor between employees of traditional international airlines and those of the expanding domestic airlines. Without a unified voice, organized labor has had little influence on international aviation liberalization.

Proposals to open domestic air service markets to foreign-owned airlines are likely to evoke a more unified labor response. Concerns over the impact of low-wage Asian labor and competition from subsidized foreign competitors are by no means limited to employees in goods-producing industries. But permitting foreign airlines to establish operations in the U.S. domestic market would not exempt those airlines from U.S. immigration or labor laws. Like Japanese automobile manufacturers with plants in the United States, foreign airlines would have to hire U.S. workers to conduct their operations and could not import cheaper foreign labor. Since domestic air services have historically accounted for almost 90 percent of total U.S. airline revenues, permitting foreign ownership of U.S. airlines is unlikely to pose a serious threat to U.S. airline labor.

In Europe the situation may be more complicated. The relatively high wages and political strength of organized labor in Europe, plus the fact that a significantly larger fraction of European carrier revenues is derived from international rather than domestic services, suggest that labor could be a more potent force in the internal European politics of liberalization. Nonetheless, the impending establishment of an internal EC common market will eventually force Europe to develop some form of a common internal labor market. By then, European domestic traffic will constitute a far larger proportion of total European airline traffic (and revenues). Thus, organized labor will find itself in much the same position as the unionized U.S. airline work force: Foreign airlines operating domestic European air services will be required to use European labor.

GOVERNMENT OWNERSHIP OR SUBSIDY

National Flag Airline

A national airline is sometimes viewed by its home government as an instrument of national policy important enough to justify financial or other protection to carry out its role, whether that role is to show the flag, to maintain sufficient capacity to satisfy national defense requirements, to develop modern technological skills in the indigenous population or to be a source of employment. A number of countries have cited the importance of the flag carrier as a reason for refusing to liberalize their international air services agreement with the United States. By subsidizing their airlines that compete in international markets, however, governments distort normal economic forces.

State ownership and subsidization of airlines may prove to be the most obstinate barrier to liberalized trade in air services because it discourages acceptance of greater liberalization by both the public and the private sectors. Governments that consider their airlines to be instruments of national policy often fear that the increased competition which would arise from liberalization would endanger the survival of their national flag airlines. Other governments resist liberalization in order to cross-subsidize airline services through higher fares rather than through budgetary appropriations.

Management and labor unions at state-owned airlines may also be less than enthusiastic about trading the shelter of the state for the uncertainties of a more competitive marketplace. They are skeptical that their government would permit the abandonment of routes, reductions in employment, lowering of wages, and other steps necessary to make the airlines competitive in a more open trading regime.

Investor-owned airlines in the United States also question the willingness of foreign governments to eliminate subsidies and other supports for their national flag carriers, and argue that liberalizing trade with such airlines is like asking U.S. carriers to "engage in a bleeding contest with a blood bank."[5] Excluding foreign carriers from the U.S. domestic markets and limiting their access to U.S. gateways are viewed as countervailing protections against unfair competition from government-supported airlines.

National Security

Many nations implicitly or explicitly depend upon the airlift capacity of the nation's airlines to meet national security airlift requirements. Israel's reliance on El Al aircraft and crews is a prime example of the defense role of the civil air fleet among noncommunist nations. In the United States, the Civil Reserve Air Fleet (CRAF) program uses preferential allocation of military cargo and passenger transport business to induce voluntary commitment of aircraft and crews for meeting emergency national security airlift requirements. Further, under the National Defense Production Act, the president can enlist all U.S. registered aircraft to meet national defense airlift requirements. Thus, national security is sometimes cited as justification for national regulatory policies that prevent or restrict competition by foreign airlines.

Upon closer examination, however, the national security argument appears to be considerably overblown. First, relatively few developed nations have national territorial or defense commitments requiring extensive long-haul airlift capability. Second, under virtually any foreseeable economic circumstances that would accompany significant liberalization of trade in air services, the nations that do have such obligations—the United States, France, the United Kingdom, Canada, and Australia—as well as other major nations such as West Germany, and Japan, among others, would retain substantial airlift capacity. Finally, nations could, if necessary, agree to maintain national aircraft registration requirements sufficient to ensure that aircraft would be available to meet essential national security objectives.

Conclusions

The barriers to further liberalization in the air services are formidable. In addition to those explicitly or implicitly created by existing bilateral air services agreements, others are embedded deep in many countries' national economic, political, and legal fabrics.

Since bilateral restrictions have already been discussed in previous international trade negotiations, they may be the easiest barriers for negotiators to overcome. As will be discussed more fully in the following chapter, however, an attempt to reduce these barriers multilaterally—particularly through the application of the GATT principles of most favored nation and national treatment—would retard rather than accelerate further liberalization in air services.

The emerging importance of network economies in the airline industry, coupled with the political necessity of assuring fair and equivalent market access for airlines from the more liberal nations, makes it imperative that future negotiations to liberalize air services directly confront barriers arising from practices historically far removed from GATT trade negotiations. These areas include domestic policies and regulations that prevent the entry and establishment of foreign firms in domestic markets; market structure, competitive conditions, and regulatory policies in an array of important ancillary markets; and the thorny issue of government ownership and subsidization.

The following chapter examines the possibilities and limitations of using the existing bilateral regime to liberalize air services; Chapter 6 analyzes the strengths and weaknesses of applying the multilateral GATT approach to air services.

NOTES

1. Examples cited in this chapter are drawn from cases dealt with by the author while serving as director of international aviation for the U.S. Civil Aeronautics Board.

2. Testimony of Marvin Cohen, chairman of the U.S. Civil Aeronautics Board, before the House Subcommittee on Investigations of the Committee on Public Works, "A Review of International Aviation Policy," 97th Cong., 1st and 2d sess., July 28–31, 1981, p. 70.
3. Testimony of John J. Casey, president of Braniff International, before the House Subcommittee on Investigations of the Committee on Public Works, "A Review of International Aviation Policy," 97th Cong., 1st and 2d sess., July 28–31, 1981, pp. 61–68.
4. The material for this section is drawn from CAB Bureau of International Aviation, "U.K. Airport User Charges," 1981.
5. Statement made to author in 1981 by John Ash, senior vice president of TWA.

5

EXPORTING COMPETITION
The U.S. Experience

Careful analysis of U.S. efforts to export competition in air services could prove instructive for future efforts to liberalize trade in air and other services. In particular, a case study of the struggle set off by American bilateral efforts to open the North Atlantic (U.S.-European) and transpacific markets to increased competition should help policymakers anticipate and utilize the interactions among domestic regulatory policies and industry economics, as well as pressures from domestic and international interest groups, to develop effective sectoral negotiating strategies.

EUROPE: ACTION AND REACTION

Britain's renunciation of its aviation agreement with the United States triggered a series of events that culminated with the 1978 adoption by the United States of a new, competitive international aviation policy and the virtual deregulation of the North Atlantic air services market by 1982.

In 1976 the British government renounced the Bermuda I air services agreement with the United States, claiming that it imposed increasingly severe competitive disadvantages on British carriers which the United States was unwilling to rectify by modifying the agreement. British negotiators identified three major problems: U.S. carrier capacity, the limited number of U.S. gateways to which British carriers had access, and the extensive U.S.-carrier traffic rights beyond London that enabled U.S.

airlines to transport local traffic between London and points throughout Europe, Asia, and the Middle East.

The Bermuda II agreement, signed in 1977, replaced the renounced agreement, and set off a furor in America because it cut back existing services to major U.S. cities (such as Boston) and reduced or eliminated the possibility that additional U.S. cities could receive nonstop service to the U.K. just when such services were becoming technically and economically viable. As a result, Bermuda II sharply increased political pressure within the United States for a more open international aviation regime. (The British renunciation also served as a reminder that an important bargaining consideration is to keep what one already has.)

The public outcry against Bermuda II prompted congressional hearings to press for changes. In addition, the success of Laker's low-fare service between New York and London spurred interest in changing the agreement to permit expansion of low-fare service. Ultimately, Civil Aeronautics Board Chairman Fred Kahn announced a new U.S. international aviation policy. Henceforth, the United States would seek to trade opportunities for opportunities, not restrictions for restrictions.

In 1978 the United States thus adopted a strategy formulated to open international air services to greater competition. Under an international aviation policy designed to "encourage vigorous competition,"[1] the Carter administration initiated an effort to expand competition in U.S. international air services markets. Since the United States held extensive route rights—particularly Third- and Fourth-Freedom rights—under its existing air services agreements, U.S. negotiators offered foreign nations access to new American gateways in exchange for Fifth-Freedom rights for U.S. airlines. U.S. negotiators also sought changes that would eliminate government restrictions on airline price competition and on the capacity to be offered on U.S. international routes. The strategy was to negotiate liberal agreements with several countries in Europe, thereby threatening to divert a substantial volume of price-sensitive traffic away from restrictive countries and their national flag carriers.[2]

European airlines generally opposed U.S. efforts to increase competition in international aviation markets, and most obtained protection from their governments against heightened competition. But this protection was far from complete. Since passengers (and cargo) between the United States and Europe can easily move via surface transport within Europe, even flag carriers in European states that strongly opposed deregulation (such as France and Germany) could be affected if price competition at other European gateways diverted or threatened to divert traffic through alternative gateways.

One of the principal functions of the International Air Transport Association (IATA) had been to develop a fare structure that minimized the threat of traffic diversion based on price competition. The plan IATA devised for fares across the North Atlantic maintained certain fare differentials among groupings of European gateways. These differentials were carefully negotiated to ensure that passengers traveling from France to New York would not fly via Amsterdam or Brussels (rather than via Paris) simply to benefit from lower ticket prices.

IATA agreements did not eliminate locational advantages. British carriers could not be expected to accept a fare structure that would eliminate all advantage arising from their nation's location vis-à-vis Europe and the United States. Rather, IATA permitted airlines to agree to a price structure that balanced, for example, Britain's superior location for U.S.-Europe traffic against France's advantage for U.K.-Africa traffic. By including virtually all prospective competitors in its pricing agreements, IATA thus minimized the risk that a carrier seeking advantage in one market would trigger a worldwide price war.

Against this delicately balanced structure, the United States aimed the first thrust of its new competitive international aviation policy. The Netherlands figured prominently in the U.S. strategy. Holland's small size made it impossible for KLM, the Dutch airline, to achieve scale economies necessary to compete effectively against airlines from Germany and France. Therefore KLM had developed a strong hub-and-spoke system that carried a substantial amount of non-Dutch traffic. Combining its well-developed European route system with expanded access to the U.S. market would allow KLM to compete more effectively with other European airlines, particularly for European-originating traffic. In addition, the Netherlands had demonstrated a strong interest in expanding access to additional U.S. gateways. If Holland would accept a liberal pricing structure and grant extensive Fifth-Freedom rights to U.S. airlines, the influx of low-fare traffic would also threaten Britain's position as the largest initial destination for U.S.-Europe travel.

Thus, when the United States signed liberal agreements with Holland, Belgium, and Israel,[3] other nations—particularly Germany and the United Kingdom—were forced to seek new agreements with the United States to keep their national airlines competitive. The U.S. strategy of liberalizing North Atlantic air services through "beachhead" agreements and the threat of diversion bore quick results. West Germany was particularly concerned about possible KLM inroads on Lufthansa's U.S.-Germany traffic and entered bilateral negotiations with the United States. Faced with the prospect that a number of liberal agreements and strong airlines would undercut British carriers' traffic as well as London's status as the principal gateway to Europe, the United Kingdom agreed to open negotiations aimed at revising the recently negotiated Bermuda II agreement. By mid-1980, both the Federal Republic of Germany and the United Kingdom had signed more liberal agreements with the United States.[4]

The pressures brought to bear on European nations and their airlines by the liberal bilaterals soon combined with the threat of another U.S. initiative, the IATA Show Cause case, to spark a European multilateral response. In June of 1978, the U.S. CAB had initiated a review of IATA's antitrust immunity. Based on an extensive analysis by the board's staff, the order directed interested parties to "show cause" why the grant of immunity should not be revoked, creating, in effect, a rebuttable presumption that the immunity was not warranted or required. The case marked the first comprehensive review of IATA's immunity since it was conferred in 1946.[5]

The potential loss of antitrust immunity was viewed with alarm by IATA and many of its airline members. Without antitrust immunity, U.S. carriers were unlikely to participate in IATA, thereby creating a twofold problem for that organization:

- U.S. carrier participation was essential if IATA agreements involving U.S. markets were to be effective. This was particularly true for the large North Atlantic and transpacific markets, in which IATA tariff agreements could not be made effective without U.S. carrier concurrence.
- Since U.S. carriers were among the largest airlines in IATA, their withdrawal from the organization would seriously undermine IATA's financial viability. (Pan American's withdrawal for several years did create some financial difficulties for IATA.)

The Show Cause order galvanized IATA and many of its member airlines to action. IATA reviewed its own rules, processes, and procedures, and changed those about which the CAB had indicated concerns.[6] Based on these "reforms" (such as the elimination of the unanimity requirements for reaching tariff agreements), IATA urged the CAB to renew its antitrust immunity. IATA also capitalized on the concern of many nations with the spreading impact of U.S. efforts to increase competition in international air service markets, and orchestrated an international campaign of diplomatic protest and pressure aimed at forcing the CAB to renew IATA's immunity. In 1979 the CAB held extensive public hearings and meetings on several continents and indicated that it would renew the immunity for IATA's facilitation activities (such as baggage handling, ticketing, etc.) while it continued to consider the question of immunity for IATA's joint rate-making activities.

The CAB issued a tentative decision in 1980 extending IATA's immunity for facilitation and other trade association activities. But the Board also concluded that the arguments raised by IATA and its supporters were not sufficient to justify the continuation of antitrust immunity for price-setting activities. In deference to the views expressed by other nations and parties, however, the CAB proposed to withdraw antitrust immunity only from the North Atlantic markets, where Laker's entry had already precipitated the collapse of the IATA conference. The

Board further limited the withdrawal of immunity to U.S. carriers.[7]

By early 1981 a final order had not yet been issued. In the interval, a number of developments occurred that would have a significant impact on the U.S. efforts to liberalize the market for air services between Europe and the United States and that would ultimately lead to a new multilateral agreement governing certain aspects of international air services.

Following the election of Ronald Reagan, incumbent U.S. international airlines had mounted a major campaign to persuade the incoming Reagan administration to abandon the Carter administration's competitive international policy.[8] In this respect, the interests of the U.S. incumbent international airlines dovetailed neatly with those of IATA: by neutralizing the American effort to export air services competition, both groups would benefit. These efforts were strongly opposed by a group of U.S. airlines actively seeking to enter international markets for the first time (such as United) or had recently been allowed to enter international scheduled service markets (Transamerica, World, and Air Florida, for example).[9]

Although the Reagan administration did not reject the competitive aviation policy, the Department of Transportation nonetheless made a concerted effort beginning in early 1981 to prevent the CAB from finalizing the IATA Show Cause order. The DoT argued that even a limited withdrawal of immunity would damage U.S. aviation and other relations with foreign nations and would undercut efforts to negotiate with European nations. Regarding the latter point, the DoT pointed to a recent offer by the European Civil Aviation Conference, or ECAC (a body composed of the aviation authorities of more than twenty European nations), to open negotiations with the United States in exchange for withdrawal of the IATA Show Cause order and renewal of IATA's antitrust immunity.[10] The CAB, however, was unwilling to give up the Show Cause case for only the promise to negotiate and insisted that substantive concessions should be obtained from the Europeans, particularly in the area of guaranteed pricing flexibility. Despite strong pressure from the DoT, the

CAB was preparing to finalize the Show Cause order and partially withdraw IATA's immunity in the late spring of 1981.

The internal U.S. government deadlock was broken by an agreement to respond to an ECAC discussion as if it were a formal proposal. Thus, the United States indicated a willingness to extend IATA's antitrust immunity in return for ECAC member states' acceptance of large double-disapproval pricing zones for international air services to and from the United States.

Nonetheless, the CAB issued an order finalizing the Show Cause order and renewing IATA's antitrust immunity, subject to certain conditions, including prohibiting U.S. carriers from participating in North Atlantic traffic conferences.[11] To give negotiators time to reach an agreement, however, the Board's order temporarily stayed the effective date of the part of the order that withdrew immunity for U.S. airlines to participate in joint rate-setting on the North Atlantic.

In mid-1982, slightly more than one year after the talks began, negotiators representing ECAC and the United States signed a new multilateral agreement.[12] This agreement provided for European acceptance of double-disapproval pricing zones in return for the CAB's renewal (for the duration of the U.S.-ECAC agreement) of the antitrust immunity for IATA's joint rate-making activities on the North Atlantic. The agreement also provided that more liberal bilateral pricing articles would prevail over the less liberal provisions of the U.S.-ECAC accord. The size of the zones and the levels of initial fares to which the zones applied were negotiated bilaterally. Methods for adjusting these zones and fares, however, were not agreed upon, and the issue was left for consideration at the time of renewal.

Although the ECAC agreement lessened the friction between the United States and some European nations (for example, France), that reduction appears to have come principally at the expense of U.S. carriers wanting to charge fares below the agreed-upon zones. Since the zones generally cover the higher fare levels preferred by many European carriers, the agreement deprived U.S. aviation authorities of some negotiating leverage vis-à-vis restrictive governments by limiting its unilateral right to disapprove a foreign carrier's tariff filing. Competition from more open markets, however, has limited the ability of even restrictive country carriers to increase fare levels.

American negotiators have also been unhappy with the process of continually renegotiating reference fare levels. In the U.S. view, European governments (and airlines) seek to increase the reference fares (and thereby the floors of the zone) without regard to whether input costs, revenues, and exchange rates justify increases. In reality, U.S.-ECAC agreement has drawn the governments into the equivalent of an IATA tariff conference. Recently, U.S. negotiators have indicated publicly that renewal of the agreement is a matter of indifference to them.

JAPAN AND ASIA

Based on the size and strength of their domestic economies, the large air travel market between the countries, and Japan's strategic location astride the Asian mainland, air services between the United States and Japan have long been regarded as the key to more competitive transpacific air services markets. Since the withdrawal of U.S. occupation forces from Japan, however, U.S.-Japanese aviation relations have been contentious.

The U.S.-Japan Air Transport Agreement, signed in 1952, was modeled after the U.S.-U.K. (Bermuda I) air services agreement.[13] The Bermuda I–style agreement contains a capacity article permitting each airline to set its own level of capacity, subject to ex post facto bilateral government review. Prices can be disapproved unilaterally by either government. Similarly, the U.S.-Japan agreement provides for multiple designations—that is, multiple airlines are authorized to provide service between the territories of the parties. There are two routes for each party, one via the North Pacific and a second via the Central Pacific. Both U.S. routes contain open-beyond rights from Tokyo, but Japan has few beyonds from the United States.

Since the late 1950s, Japan has repeatedly argued that the agreement favored the United States. Indeed, Japan complained that the United States had imposed the agreement on Japan, and that Japan would not have accepted it had the postwar bargaining power of the parties been equal. In stark contrast to the U.S. desire for increased competition in U.S.-Japan air services, Japan forcefully advocated a restrictive international aviation policy with tightly regulated airlines and severely limited competition.

Throughout the postwar period, Japanese negotiators have attempted to tie virtually every new exercise of bilateral rights by the United States to an increase in operating rights for Japanese carriers. Japan has focused attention on the number of U.S. airlines serving Japan, the capacity they offer, and the extensive Fifth-Freedom rights that permit U.S. carriers to offer service from Japan throughout Asia. Thus, any major change in operations proposed by U.S. carriers has required extended consultations and negotiations between the governments.

Shortly after the United States adopted its competitive international aviation policy in 1978, the U.S. CAB issued a decision in a decade-old route case by selecting United Airlines to serve Japan via Seattle and Portland.[14] Almost simultaneously, Continental/Air Micronesia sought an increase in its service from Saipan/Guam to Japan. Meanwhile, a strong counterattack was mounted by U.S. incumbent airlines (Flying Tigers, Northwest Orient, and Pan American) that opposed United's entry into the U.S.-Japan market and sought to prevent or delay that carrier's designation.

To overcome Japan's opposition to increased competition in the Pacific basin aviation market, the United States adopted a three-pronged strategy:[15]

1. Encircle Japan with liberal, competitive markets to divert traffic from Tokyo. Since 1978, the United States had negotiated new, liberal agreements with Korea, the Philippines, Thailand, Singapore, and Taiwan.[16]
2. Exercise bilateral rights, including the designation of United Airlines to service Seattle-Tokyo, Continental/Air Micronesia to serve an additional city in Japan, and Pan American to serve China via Tokyo.

3. Open negotiations with Japan to revise the postwar air services agreement. Here the aim was to meet Japan's growth objectives as well as those of the United States.

The proposed services by United Airlines, Air Micronesia, and Pan American were expected to revive Japanese complaints that the agreement favored the United States, but U.S. analysis of traffic data refuted the Japanese contention. For calendar year 1979, the three U.S. carriers providing passenger service in the U.S.-Japan market divided 47 percent of the scheduled passenger traffic, while Japan Airlines carried 46 percent. Third-country airlines carried the remainder.[17]

In addition, Pan American's proposed service to China via Tokyo was certain to rekindle Japanese complaints about the disparity between the Fifth-Freedom operations by U.S. carriers beyond Japan and the limited rights of Japanese carriers beyond the United States. Most U.S. carrier flights to Japan went beyond to other countries, and Japan contended that U.S. carrier Fifth-Freedom traffic beyond Japan was greatly disproportionate to the Third- and Fourth-Freedom traffic. But in those same markets (the Hong Kong–U.S. route, for example), JAL carried large amounts of traffic to and from the United States, traffic it refused to consider in measuring its benefits under the bilateral.[18] Japan could attempt to correct the perceived imbalance in two ways. It could press for a reduction of U.S. rights (especially Fifth Freedom) or for an increase in Japanese route rights.

Despite the historically troubled U.S.-Japanese aviation relations, economic and political conditions in 1980 promised at least some hope for progress in negotiations to liberalize the existing air services regime. Japan had a (then) huge $8.6 billion trade surplus with the United States in 1979, which was forecast to increase to almost $10 billion in 1980. The impending threat of U.S. automobile import quotas suggested that Japanese agreement to open the U.S.-Japan air services market would be a highly visible and relatively low-cost way to show commitment to an open trading system.

There were also indications that the protectionistic influence of Japan Air Lines on Japan's negotiating posture might be waning. The progress that All Nippon Airways, Japan's largest airline, appeared to be making in its attempt to break JAL's monopoly on international services increased the Japanese negotiators' interest in pursuing expanded access for their nation's carriers to the large U.S. market. (All Nippon's earlier efforts to obtain international rights had been stymied by allegations that the carrier had been involved in the Lockheed bribery scandal.)

The U.S. negotiators were convinced that the existing agreement required Japan to accept the new U.S. carrier services, but they also had a strong sense that unless the United States responded to Japan's concerns about the imbalance of route rights under that agreement, either the United Airlines Seattle-Tokyo route or the continuance of the existing agreement, or both, would be jeopardized. Thus the delegation developed a proposal featuring a large "carrot" for Japan—significant expansion of its existing route and beyond-traffic rights. Since the United States, too, sought changes in the agreement, U.S. negotiators proposed to satisfy most of Japan's route objectives if Japan would agree to substantial liberalization in such areas as pricing, charters, and access. The proposal was tabled at the opening round of talks at Honolulu in January 1981.

The Japanese response to the U.S. proposal almost scuttled the negotiations. As the incumbent U.S. airlines lobbied heavily for America to withdraw its concessions, Japan counteroffered a proposal that satisfied virtually all of Japan's objectives and none of the aims of the United States. This counterproposal fueled the campaign of the U.S. incumbent airlines against the liberal aviation policy and induced some of them to seek a pullback of the opening U.S. offer. The first round of talks adjourned without agreement.

After several additional rounds had failed, and with no agreement in sight, United filed an unfair competitive practices complaint with the CAB based upon Japan's failure to grant the operating authority necessary for United to begin service to Japan.[19] The complaint asked the Board to impose sanctions on JAL that would restrict that carrier's access to the lucrative New York gateway. Incumbent U.S. airlines serving Japan, however, filed pleadings in opposition to the request for sanctions, and one incumbent (Northwest) even argued that the Japanese had not violated U.S. bilateral rights by refusing to authorize service by United. The CAB temporarily deferred final action on United's complaint while the United States and Japan explored possible avenues for resolving the underlying dispute. Further negotiations were eventually scheduled, less than one month before the board's statutory deadline for acting on United's complaint.[20]

When this round, too, ended without agreement, the Board issued its decision on the United complaint. In its order, the CAB found that Japan had "committed a serious violation" of the air services agreement in refusing to authorize United's service to Japan. The Board imposed a number of minor sanctions on JAL (such as deferring action on pending JAL applications) but also required JAL to file its schedules with the CAB, a formality required before the Board could order a reduction in a carrier's service. More importantly, the Board submitted to President Reagan for his approval a confidential order imposing additional, more severe sanctions against JAL. The order also contained a recommendation that the additional sanctions be temporarily deferred to give the negotiators a final chance to reach agreement.[21] The Japanese government responded by imposing a number of largely prospective sanctions against U.S. carriers serving Japan. For example, no action would be taken on requests by U.S. carriers to initiate new services beyond Tokyo. The stakes had now become higher.

A "final" round of negotiations had apparently reached an agreement when a critical story (reportedly planted by a senior JAL executive) appeared in the Tokyo press and ruptured the fragile consensus between the Japanese Transport Ministry and the Ministry of Foreign Affairs. Intensive lobbying by U.S. airlines in Washington left the U.S. delegation, too, with little room to maneuver, and the talks collapsed. Within a week, however, intensive talks had resumed in Washington between the Japanese ambassador and the chairman of the U.S. delegation. Over the objections of the U.S. airlines (including United), a temporary agreement was reached. Pending completion or breakdown of new negotiations to revise the U.S.-Japan air services agreement, United was authorized to operate daily service between Seattle and Portland and Tokyo, Continental/Air Micronesia gained access to Nagoya, and JAL obtained new access to Chicago and Seattle.[22]

Further bilateral negotiations since 1983 have led to the authorization of additional services between the United States and Japan. To date, American Airlines, Delta, All Nippon, Nippon All Cargo Airlines, and JAL have introduced new services. New all-cargo (small-package express) services have also been authorized, but not yet begun, for one U.S. airline. Federal Express has been selected to provide that service.

THE CONTINUING AFTERSHOCKS OF U.S. DEREGULATION

Despite the Reagan administration's somewhat less aggressive efforts to negotiate liberal air services agreements, the ripple effects of U.S. airline deregulation continue to cause major changes in the airline industry, both domestically and worldwide. Of particular significance is the large-scale invasion of international markets by the largest and strongest U.S. airlines. In addition to United, American, and Delta's institution of new services to Japan and other Asian points, acquisitions and mergers are redefining the competitive landscape. United, for instance, acquired Pan American's Pacific route system in 1985. With its extensive domestic route network, United is a significantly more formidable competitor for Asian airlines than was Pan American with its weak domestic route system. The subsequent merger of Republic Airlines into Northwest similarly strengthened Northwest's position to compete for traffic to and from Asia.

The transatlantic market has witnessed a similar expansion by U.S. airlines, particularly those that had been restricted to domestic operations prior to deregulation. American Airlines, for example, has instituted new nonstop services to various European destinations from Dallas, Chicago, New York, and Raleigh-Durham. Delta serves Europe from Atlanta, Dallas, and Cincinnati, while Continental serves Europe from Newark,

Miami, Houston, and Denver. Piedmont's recent introduction of London-Charlotte service leaves United as the only major U.S. carrier without scheduled service to Europe. As discussed in Chapter 2, however, United has entered into a major joint marketing agreement with British Airways.

The rapid international expansion of deregulated U.S. airlines has simultaneously increased U.S. carrier competitiveness and, by reducing the availability of domestic airlines to provide connections to and from behind-gateway points in the United States, diminished that of foreign airlines. This, in turn, has led to substantial liberalization of domestic and international aviation regulation outside of the United States, as foreign governments seek to replicate efficiency gains enjoyed by U.S. airlines. It has also increased foreign government pressure on the United States to grant their carriers greater access to the U.S. market, as well as induced some implied threats to reduce U.S. carrier rights if negotiations fail to arrive at an acceptable balance. It may also be responsible for an apparent increase in questionable foreign competitive practices—such as measures blocking the use of U.S. carrier CRS systems in foreign markets.

As will be discussed in Chapter 6, however, granting foreign access to the internal U.S. market poses complex problems for U.S. negotiators. Even if existing legislation were amended to permit foreign airlines to carry domestic traffic, three difficult problems would remain:

1. To compete on even terms with domestic carriers in the large U.S. market, foreign airlines might have to provide connecting service (via their U.S. gateways) to numerous interior U.S. points. The expense of acquiring and operating a fleet of aircraft sufficient to cover the U.S. market, however, would require that the aircraft be used substantially more than would be necessary to provide international connecting service. In short, to compete actively for international traffic to and from the United States would likely require the right to establish or acquire, and operate an airline in the U.S. domestic market.

2. If foreign airlines are given the right of establishment in the United States, U.S. carriers must also be given that right in foreign markets to ensure that all carriers enjoy equivalent access to traffic on both ends of the route. No single nation in Europe or Asia, however, can provide a large internal market or geographic expanse equivalent to those of the U.S. market. The economic equivalent of the U.S. internal market is not access to, say, the United Kingdom or Germany but access to all of Western Europe. Currently, Europe lacks an institution capable of negotiating such comparable access.
3. Before authorizing U.S. negotiators to permit foreign airlines to carry domestic traffic or establish operations in the United States, Congress is likely to insist on satisfactory measures to eliminate unfair competitive practices and other barriers to effective access by U.S. carriers (see Chapter 6). Since many of these barriers involve sensitive issues of national policy and politics such negotiations are likely to be complex and contentious.

CONCLUSIONS

After almost a decade of bilateral efforts to export deregulation and liberalization of air services, what conclusions can be drawn from the U.S. experience? Three observations have particular relevance to the forthcoming GATT services round.

First, achieving significant liberalization is possible, even in a bilateral regime, by using the "carrot" of access to large, economically attractive markets and the "stick" of diversion. The threat of diversion creates a prisoners' dilemma for those opposed to liberalization, while the prospect of access to a large, attractive market can attract those nations that favor liberalization.

Second, the use of such carrot-and-stick tactics to wean an industry away from a comfortable regulatory pattern is certain to trigger significant international and domestic resistance. To prevail against the defenders of the status quo, it is essential to understand and utilize the underlying economic forces affecting the industry.

Third, disparities in national boundaries and market sizes severely limit the efficacy of bilateralism as a vehicle for liberalizing trade in air (and other) services. The United States has largely exhausted the air services liberalizations attainable bilaterally. Further significant liberalizations are thus likely to require multilateral negotiations.

NOTES

1. "United States Policy for the Conduct of International Air Transportation Negotiations," Executive Office of the President, August 21, 1978.
2. D. Kasper, "Deregulation and Its Impact on Pacific Aviation" (Speech to the Chicago World Trade Conference, April 18, 1985).
3. 1978 Protocol to the 1957 Air Services Agreement between the Kingdom of the Netherlands and the United States of America, T.I.A.S. 8998; 1980 Air Services Agreement between Belgium and the United States of America, T.I.A.S. 9903; 1978 Protocol to the 1950 Air Services Agreement between Israel and the United States of America, T.I.A.S. 9002.
4. T.I.A.S. 9591 (FRG) and 8641 (U.K.).
5. Docket 32851 CAB, Order 78-6-78, June 9, 1978.
6. Docket 32851, Order 80-4-113, April 15, 1980.
7. Ibid.
8. Testimony of Pan American Chairman William Seawell before the House Subcommittee on Investigations of the Committee on Public Works, "A Review of U.S. International Aviation Policy," 97th Cong., 1st and 2nd sess., July 28, 1981, pp. 69 et seq.
9. Testimony of Edward J. Driscoll before the House Subcommittee on Investigations of the Committee on Public Works, "A Review of U.S. International Aviation Policy," 97th Cong., July 28, 1981, pp. 477ff.
10. Author's contemporaneous notes.
11. CAB Docket 32851, Order 81-5-27.
12. U.S. ECAC Memorandum of Understanding, May 2, 1982.

13. 1953 Air Transport Agreement between Japan and the United States of America, T.I.A.S. 2854.
14. *Seattle/Portland-Japan Service Investigation*, CAB Order 78-10-42, July 6, 1987.
15. Kasper, "Deregulation."
16. T.I.A.S. 9427 (Korea), 10443 (Philippines), 9704 (Thailand), 9654 (Singapore); AIT-CCNAA Air Services Agreement (Taiwan).
17. Civil Aeronautics Board, Bureau of International Aviation, Staff Analysis of U.S.-Japan Traffic, July 1980 (internal memo).
18. Ibid. Japan argued since that traffic was not subject to the U.S.-Japan agreement, it should not be counted in determining bilateral balance. See also Chapter 3, note 7.
19. Complaint of United Airlines, Inc., against the Japanese Civil Aviation Bureau and Japan Air Lines, Co. Ltd., CAB Docket 39710, June 15, 1981.
20. CAB Docket 39710, Order 81-12-91, December 14, 1981.
21. Ibid.
22. U.S.-Japan, Record of Consultations, signed on June 4, 1982.

6

AIR SERVICES AND THE GATT

The United States approaches the Uruguay Round from a position of strength in the air services sector. With unrestricted access to a large deregulated domestic market and, through liberal international agreements, to substantial international markets as well, U.S. airlines enjoy a uniquely strong position among the world's airlines. By exploiting the significant economies of scope and scale available to airlines with extensive networks, a relatively small group of U.S. mega-carriers has begun to invade international markets. Strengthened by the rigors of deregulated competition in the U.S. market, these American carriers are now increasing competition in international airline markets around the globe.

Yet America faces a dilemma in considering further air services liberalization. Although its airlines could be expected to benefit from expanded access to worldwide markets, the price for such access is certain to involve expanded foreign access to the U.S. domestic market. Under the prevailing bilateral system, however, it is virtually impossible for other nations to provide sufficient access for U.S. carriers to justify opening the U.S. domestic market. Since the economic equivalent of access to the internal U.S. market would involve, for example, comparable access for U.S. carriers in the intra-Europe market, further liberalization will almost certainly require some type of multilateral agreement.

The GATT is an obvious vehicle for reaching such an agreement, but certainly not the only one. Nor would the application of the GATT to air services be free of difficulty. In particular, applying key GATT principles including unconditional most-favored-nation and national treatment could actually impede further liberalization rather than enhance it. This chapter reviews the key principles upon which the GATT multilateral approach to trade liberalization is erected and explores their strengths and weaknesses when applied to air services.

TRANSPARENCY

Because trade barriers must be identified before they can be eliminated and to discourage the erection of new barriers, GATT signatories are encouraged to make any barriers to trade, whether intended as such or adopted for other reasons, "transparent," or obvious, to the world. The obligation to provide public notification of laws, regulations, and practices that affect foreign suppliers of services is thus envisioned by most observers as a central component of a services agreement.[1]

The explicit adoption of a transparency principle would present no significant problems in the context of air services. Indeed, transparency has been endorsed by the United States and the European Civil Aviation Conference in the U.S.-ECAC agreement described in Chapter 5.

Even with a principle as unassailable as transparency, however, some negotiating caution is advisable. In the U.S.-ECAC air service negotiations, for example, ECAC's initial interest in transparency appeared to be motivated more by a desire to delay and restrain U.S. procompetitive initiatives on the North Atlantic than by a desire to further the liberalization of international air services.

Caution is also warranted in evaluating the suggestion that parties be exempted from retaliation for maintaining trade barriers if those barriers were publicly identified prior to a specified date.[2] Such an "immunity for transparency" approach explicitly legitimizes the barriers as bargaining chips and misdirects the focus of negotiations on eliminating specific barriers rather than on ensuring comparable market access. The central importance of networks in air services makes equivalent access—

not equivalent reductions in barriers—the crucial negotiating objective.

MOST FAVORED NATION (MFN)

The core of the GATT trading system is the concept of nondiscrimination. Article I of the GATT promulgates a rule of unconditional most favored nation (MFN), which requires GATT contracting parties to apply any trade concessions equally to imports, regardless of their source. That is, all contracting parties are entitled to the same treatment as that accorded to the most favored nation. The GATT does not preclude more limited trade agreements, such as bilateral accords, but instead requires that any concessions contained in such agreements be applied equally to all GATT signatories.

For air services, a distinction can be drawn between the application of MFN to economic rights—particularly routes, capacity, and pricing—and its application in such ancillary areas as commercial operations. In the latter case, MFN would prevent a government, for example, from permitting some foreign airlines but not others to advertise and sell directly to the public. In the former, MFN would require the United States to give airlines from every nation the same degree of access to the U.S. market regardless of whether those nations had opened their markets to U.S. airlines.

Political and Economic Implications

The application of unconditional MFN to the air transport sector would create substantial political and economic problems. Indeed, the very suggestion that unconditional MFN might be applied to air services would be certain to arouse industry opposition and seriously damage the prospects for liberalization. There are several reasons for this.

First, the prospect of extending equal access to all nations without regard for or assurances of comparable access for U.S.

airlines to markets abroad would create domestic political furor. It would leave U.S. negotiators vulnerable to charges that they had not redressed the unfairness of closed foreign markets and would heighten airlines' fears that their interests would be sacrificed for those of other sectors. By automatically extending to all GATT signatories concessions made to the most liberal U.S. trading partners, unconditional MFN would also undercut significantly the U.S. market's attractiveness as a "carrot" for encouraging protectionist governments to open their markets to U.S. airlines.

Second, unconditional MFN would deprive air service negotiators of essential flexibility. Trade barriers in air services vary widely in form and impact across markets, forcing even liberal nations to discriminate when granting traffic rights in order to counteract the sometimes severe restraints their carriers encounter in foreign markets. Due to the nature of these nontarrif barriers and to the fact that they often arise in ancillary markets, a universal solution, such as the elimination of the ancillary restraints by all signatories, would be exceedingly difficult to negotiate and to enforce.

Under these circumstances, adopting unconditional MFN would undermine the ability of governments to tailor packages of economic rights that offset the mix of restraints in particular foreign markets. It would be especially troubling for those markets characterized by a high degree of cooperation between the national airline and the government.

Third, the U.S. airlines and Congress have already expressed doubts about the adequacy of even the bilateral system (and, occasionally, the willingness of U.S. government agencies) to protect U.S. carriers from unfair competitive practices by foreign governments. It seems highly unlikely that either the airlines or Congress would willingly accept an MFN-based system, which necessarily curtails the ability of U.S. negotiators to adapt exchanges of substantive economic rights to correspond with the degree to which foreign markets are effectively (as opposed to nominally) open to U.S. airlines.

The increasing business and labor pressures on the Congress to protect various U.S. industries strongly suggests that the airlines' skepticism regarding the efficacy of GATT as a vehicle for protecting U.S. firms from unfair foreign competition is shared by other sectors. The concern is particularly acute regarding "plan-driven" economies such as Korea and Brazil, in which domestic firms could be regarded as vertically integrated with their governments. Under the present circumstances, it should not be surprising that U.S. airlines might equate the invitation to extend GATT's MFN principle to air services with an invitation from an obviously floundering swimmer to "come on in, the water's fine."

Finally, the competitive importance of comparable market access in industries characterized by significant network economies and other economies of scope leave the air services industry particularly vulnerable to manipulation by protectionist governments. When combined with the traditional focus of GATT negotiations on the degree by which trade barriers are reduced (rather than on comparable access), the economics of networks suggest that adopting unconditonal MFN could significantly harm U.S. firms.

Bargaining Implications

Applying unconditional MFN to air transport could also reduce the prospects for attaining a liberalizing agreement by hampering, if not altogether stifling, the bargaining process.

The danger arises from at least two sources. On a mundane level, the application of MFN would necessitate more extensive, a priori analyses of the costs and benefits of any given set of concessions. If the United States and Canada, for example, wanted to negotiate an air services common market, it would be relatively simple for the two governments and their respective airlines to estimate the prospective economic gains and losses from bilateral free trade in the air services. By automatically extending to all nations full access to U.S. and Canadian markets, however, unconditional MFN would increase the uncertainty regarding the net benefits of any agreement—at least for producers in the United States and Canada. Negotiators would have to undertake the much more complicated task of estimating the impact of granting airlines of all nations free access to the U.S. and Canadian markets. At a minimum, that process would greatly slow the negotiating process.

More important, the uncertainty surrounding the net benefits of an agreement reached subject to unconditional MFN would decrease the expected value of that agreement, particularly for politically powerful industry interests. The expected value of an air services agreement can be represented as follows:

$$V = p \times A,$$

where V = the expected value of the agreement;

p = the combined probability that the agreement will be honored and, if not, that it will be effectively enforced; and

A = the nominal value of the agreement.

For U.S. and Canadian airlines, the value of A is a function of the additional traffic made accessible by an agreement, less the cost of increased competition that would result from the agreement. By permitting third parties to expand their access to the United States and Canada without requiring those same parties to open their markets to U.S. and Canadian airlines, unconditional MFN would increase the competition faced by the North American airlines without increasing their access to new markets outside of North America.

In this situation, the United States and Canada would almost certainly be compelled to engage in multilateral negotiations in order to seek concessions from nations that would otherwise be free-rider beneficiaries of a U.S.-Canadian agreement. Since free-riders would benefit from any U.S.-Canadian agreement under unconditional MFN, however, protectionist nations have only limited incentives to make concessions that benefit the United States and Canada.

Furthermore, the expected value of concessions must be substantially discounted from their nominal value for nations whose markets are protected by a complex array of trade barriers and for those that have a poor record of compliance with their existing international obligations. (See the section on dispute settlement procedures, below.)

The GATT relies on multisectoral negotiations to resolve the externalities/free-rider issue by ensuring a "balance of concessions"—that is, the expectation that each party will have sufficient potential gains in some sectors to compensate for free-rider losses in other sectors. The notion is to reach a balance of overall benefits by expanding the scope of negotiations. GATT supporters also argue that the externalities are benefits, not costs. In the case of the United States and Canada, for example, air travelers would benefit by the opening of the markets to airlines from all GATT signatories.

But the assumption that free-rider losses in one sector will be offset by net benefits in another compounds the domestic political difficulties inherent in gaining industry support for inclusion of air services under the GATT. At best, such an approach is imprecise. At worst, it encourages nations to liberalize only to the minimum extent necessary to induce liberalization by others. The latter problem arises from applying unconditional MFN and makes the GATT a fatally flawed vehicle for liberalizing the air transport sector. Instead of awarding MFN treatment only to those nations prepared to adhere to conditions designed to ensure liberalized trade in a particular sector, unconditional MFN generalizes market-opening concessions without requiring beneficiaries to accept market liberalizing conditions. Thus, like a traditional auction, where the bidding starts low and works up, it encourages nations to offer the lowest possible "bid," or package of concessions, necessary.

By setting as its objective the liberalization of trade, rather than the attainment of a liberal trade regime, the GATT has effectively converted trade barriers into valuable bargaining chips for protectionist nations to use in fending off liberalization. A better model might be drawn from the Dutch flower-market auctions, where the price starts high and declines until a bid is received. For air services, such an approach would define a liberal regime and then extend MFN treatment only to those nations prepared to accept the entire trade-liberalizing package. Other nations might be permitted to accede on a more limited basis if they agreed to pay compensation for any derogation. Ways that such an approach might be used to liberalize trade in air services will be discussed in the following chapter.

NATIONAL TREATMENT

National treatment for services would require that foreign services and suppliers receive the same treatment as comparable domestic services and suppliers. Applying the national treatment principle to all aspects of air services would raise thorny—perhaps intractable—legal and conceptual problems.

Existing U.S. international air service agreements require nondiscrimination between U.S. and foreign airlines. Foreign airlines serving the United States are generally free to conduct their commercial operations on the same basis as U.S. airlines. That is, they are entitled to establish offices, advertise, market, provide ground-handling services for themselves and others, and, generally, to compete for traffic on the same terms as U.S. airlines.

The same conditions do not always prevail in markets outside of the United States. As described in Chapter 4, a number of governments permit or impose discrimination in such crucial areas as computer reservation systems and airport services. There are, moreover, important exceptions to this general rule of nondiscrimination, even for the United States. Agreements between the United States and countries with nonmarket economies, such as the U.S.S.R., for example, rely on strict bilateral reciprocity to protect U.S. carriers. In addition, a number of nations, including the United States, require that air transportation paid for by government funds be provided by one of that nation's flag airlines. For charter services, many nations impose a restrictive policy, requiring that local carriers be given a right of first refusal for any charter flights originating in that country. If the application of national treatment were limited to these types of doing-business issues (which often afflict other service industries as well), it could potentially deal with a significant number of nontariff barriers that impede air services liberalization.

More important, however, is the fact that nondiscrimination does not extend to key economic rights such as routes. Thus the United States is not required to permit a German airline to serve a St. Louis–Frankfurt route simply because TWA serves it. Nor would the United Kingdom be required to permit U.S. flag service between Manchester and St. Louis simply because service on that route had been instituted by a British (or a German) airline.

For domestic air services, an even more restrictive situation prevails. Airlines owned or controlled by foreign nationals are legally precluded from serving domestic air service markets in the United States and most other countries. Legislative changes would thus be required to implement a national treatment requirement for domestic air services. Application of the national treatment principle to domestic markets would raise major bargaining, economic, and political issues which are discussed in the following two sections.

Shortcomings and Bargaining Implications of National Treatment

While meaningful liberalization of trade in air services clearly will require the substantial reduction or elimination of barriers to domestic markets, governments—particularly those from countries with sizable domestic markets—have rejected proposals that would increase foreign carrier access to domestic markets. In the United States, airlines have resisted proposals to expand direct access by foreign airlines to the American market as well as suggestions that foreign carriers be permitted to acquire U.S. airlines.

In addition to some obvious protectionism, U.S. airlines have several legitimate concerns about expansion of foreign carrier access to the U.S. market. Competition in the deregulated U.S. market has demonstrated the importance of operating a widespread network of hubs, each supported by an array of flights to a multitude of destinations. The U.S. domestic market is the largest domestic air services market in the world, in terms of both traffic and geography. Since the United States permits free entry into its domestic air services market, foreign carriers given access to the U.S. domestic market have the assurance that domestic regulatory restrictions would not prevent them from establishing operations in a market large enough to support operations on an economically efficient scale.

If given access to other nations' domestic markets, in contrast, U.S. airlines would face markets too small to support efficient operations. In addition, even under the principle of national treatment, U.S. American carriers would face the same certainty of rejection as that encountered by nationals seeking to establish an airline in most nations' domestic markets.

Conflicting domestic regulatory systems thus combine with small national markets to create a significant negotiating problem for any effort to liberalize trade in air services: even if U.S. negotiators could grant access to the U.S. domestic market, no single foreign government would be in a position to provide equivalent access for the United States. In short, U.S. trading partners may not yet be capable of delivering a package of rights for the United States comparable to that which the United States can give to them. Equivalence would require, for example, assured access for U.S. airlines to the internal European market in exchange for European carrier access to the U.S. domestic market. Furthermore, U.S. airlines should also be permitted to acquire existing European airlines, and vice versa, so that investment can be at least a partial substitute for the right to enter markets.

The European Community is slowly moving toward an internal common market for air services but is not yet in a position to negotiate air services issues with the United States, much less to offer access to internal European air services markets or to permit U.S. acquisition of European airlines. As noted earlier, the United States would have to amend the Federal Aviation Act to permit foreign carriers to carry purely domestic traffic as well as to establish or acquire control of a U.S. air carrier.

Although it might be argued that the United States should open its markets notwithstanding the problems of access to foreign markets, it must be recognized that as a practical matter it would be politically infeasible for U.S. air service negotiators to repeat the now widely criticized approach used in telecommunications, where the United States first opened its market and then sought to negotiate access to foreign markets.

Given this situation, a multilateral organization like the GATT should be able to provide an institutional vehicle for aggregating a set of concessions sufficiently large to attract nations with large domestic markets. In GATT parlance, the issue is one of balancing concessions. Since the gains attainable from purely bilateral bargaining appear to have been largely exhausted, the time would appear ripe for a multilateral approach.

Nonetheless, an attempt to broadly apply the national treatment principle to air services is fraught with problems and would almost certainly exacerbate the bargaining problem rather than help to resolve it. By granting foreign carriers access to domestic markets on the same terms as local carriers, national treatment would essentially increase market access for nations with closed domestic markets without significantly expanding access for airlines whose domestic markets have already been deregulated. While national treatment would assure foreign airlines' access to the deregulated U.S. domestic air services market, it would not ease the strict limits on entry typical in foreign markets. Thus national treatment would guarantee foreign airlines entry into the U.S. market but would guarantee U.S. airlines abroad only the same certainty of rejection faced by nationals seeking to operate air services in those countries.

Extending national treatment only to nations that have deregulated domestic air service markets and opened them to entry by foreign airlines affords a partial solution to the dilemma but does little to resolve the issue of market equivalence, an acute problem for countries with large domestic markets. Given the importance of network access and economies of scope in airline markets, application of national treatment could thus put U.S. carriers at a significant competitive disadvantage. It would also invite strong domestic opposition in the United States and other countries with large domestic markets. Since the active support of these countries will be critical to any significant liberalization of the air transport sector, such an approach would seriously undermine the possibility of concluding a significant trade-liberalizing agreement. Limiting the application of national treatment to such issues as ticket sales and marketing, advertising, and access to airport and other facilities and supplies (for example, fuel) could help alleviate some of the more egregious discriminatory measures adopted by protectionist states but would do little to liberalize trade restrictions in the more important area of substantive economic rights.

Thus, national treatment is at the same time too sweeping and too limited when applied to economic rights. Its sweep is too broad since it would force nations with deregulated domestic markets to open their markets to "free-riders" with restrictive domestic regulatory market systems, and would thereby discourage more liberal nations from deregulating their domestic markets. At the same time, it is too limited in its ability to deal effectively with the problem of entry barriers and restrictive domestic regulations imposed by illiberal nations.

DISPUTE RESOLUTION

The GATT's dispute-resolution procedures are often cited as a major advantage of applying a GATT-based system to the services sector. Indeed, it would be difficult to establish a viable multilateral trade regime for services without a timely and effective dispute-resolution procedure. Although GATT dispute-resolution procedures appear to offer a significant improvement over the current process for resolving disputes in some important service sectors,[3] they may prove inadequate for sectors, such as air services, that have well-developed means for resolving disputes.[4]

Most problems under air service bilaterals are resolved at the carrier-government level or informally between governments. If such means fail, the dispute settlement procedures in U.S. air service bilaterals typically permit an aggrieved party to invoke expedited consultations within thirty to sixty days. If these consultations also fail to resolve the issue, the aggrieved party is free to submit the dispute to arbitration.

Along with a number of other nations, the United States asserts that a nation may take steps to protect its position and preserve the relative benefits derived from its agreement until a dispute arising under that agreement is resolved. Thus, the United States reserves the right to restrict the operations of a foreign airline if it determines that U.S. rights under the agreement are being abridged by that airline's national government. For an example, see the discussion of U.S.-Japan negotiations in Chapter 5.

As a practical matter, this system has led to very few arbitral proceedings. Instead, the process has encouraged dispute resolution below or, less frequently, at the political levels of government. The ability of government aviation officials to initiate retaliatory action is restrained by the bureaucratic cost of doing so. Likewise, the inconvenience caused to travelers and voters, the mutual vulnerability of airline operations to government sanctions, and the high level of political visibility inherent in retaliatory exchanges, has apparently made the cost of disagreement high enough to encourage airlines and nations to resolve their air service disputes rapidly.

Bargaining Implications

Dispute-resolution procedures are likely to be a crucial feature of any service sector agreement. In addition to providing a neutral forum for the peaceful resolution of disagreements, dispute-resolution procedures help to preserve the balance of benefits negotiated by the parties to that agreement. Moreover, the perceived effectiveness of dispute-resolution procedures is likely to play a critical role in whether an agreement is reached and the degree to which that agreement will liberalize trade.

The slower and less effective a remedy is perceived to be, the less likely it becomes that rules-abiding nations will open their markets to foreign competition. In probabilistic terms, this can be simplified as follows:

$$V = p \times A$$

where V = the discounted value of an agreement to a nation;

p = the combined probabilities that the agreement will be honored ($p1$) and effectively remedied ($p2$) (for values of $p1$ less than 1); and

A = the nominal value of the agreement.

Thus, if

A = \$1,000,000 and

p = .54 (0.9 probability of honoring × 0.6 probability of remedy),

then

V = \$540,000.

If the likelihood of breach remains the same, an increase in the likelihood of effective remedy ($p2$) to 0.9 will raise p to 0.81 and V to \$810,000. (Note the similarity here to the effects of uncertainty regarding the benefits of agreement that would result from introducing unconditional MFN into air service negotiations, discussed above.

Further, the more effective the remedy procedure (the greater the value of $p2$), the more likely it is that the agreement will be honored (the greater will be the value of $p1$). This simply reflects the fact that effective remedies reduce the benefits that might be derived from cheating.

These observations are not new. Indeed, analogous situations in torts, contracts, and criminal law have been thoroughly analyzed in such terms. Nonetheless, the implications of this analysis for attaining a liberalized agreement in air services—and possibly other sectors—may prove critical for the United States during the Uruguay Round of GATT negotiations.

Faced with a monumental trade deficit, growing protectionism, and widespread skepticism about the willingness of key trading partners to compete fairly, it is unlikely that any U.S. administration for the foreseeable future will accept an agreement that significantly increases foreign access to U.S. markets unless it contains remedies and dispute-resolution procedures that the Congress deems sufficient to deter cheating and to protect the U.S. from unfair competition. Thus, the prospective importance of remedies and dispute-resolution procedures is likely to be significantly greater than in earlier rounds when the U.S. trade position and accounts were more robust.

A ROLE FOR THE GATT?

The foregoing analysis has examined the structure of the world air services industry and the economic forces reshaping it. The study has also described the existing legal regime governing air services, identified significant barriers to the liberalization of air services, and examined bilateral approaches to liberalization. Finally, the study has evaluated the potential applicability of multilateral GATT principles and procedures to air services. What can be learned from this analysis about the potential contribution of GATT to a further liberalization of world trade in air services?

Develop Timely and Effective Remedies and Dispute-Resolution Procedures

By specifically seeking to reduce the rewards for cheating, remedial and dispute-resolution procedures could increase the expected value of agreements, particularly for rules-abiding nations. They could also contribute to the perceived fairness of an agreement, a crucial consideration in its domestic political acceptability.

This analysis suggests that by providing ready access to dispute-settlement panels that rendered prompt decisions, the GATT would enhance—perhaps substantially—both the prospects for agreement and the degree of liberalization in any bargains ultimately negotiated. It also suggests that strengthening available remedies would improve the prospects for liberalization in air and other service sectors.

The GATT appears well situated to meet both of these requirements. It is already recognized as an appropriate forum for resolving international trade disputes, and its existing dispute-resolution services provide a base for GATT to attain significant economies of scale in the provision of dispute-resolution services.

Currently, however, the GATT dispute-settlement process is neither timely nor efficient, characterized instead by delays in the formation of dispute-resolution panels, long panel deliberations, and ineffective remedies.[5] Until the GATT can assure prompt resolution of disputes and effective remedies, it is unlikely to be viewed as an attractive alternative to current practices, at least for air services.

Be Cautious about Unconditional Most-Favored-Nation and National Treatment

By introducing added complexity and uncertainty about the net benefits of agreement, particularly for nations critical to any viable multilateral air services agreement, unconditional MFN would impair, not enhance, the prospects for liberalizing air services. An earlier discussion pointed out the difficulties inherent in applying unconditional MFN to air services. Given the ease with which nominal concessions can be undercut by an array of trade barriers embedded in domestic regulatory systems, in the market structure of related industries, and in other government policies, the application of unconditional MFN would require the United States, for example, to undertake an extensive analysis of the costs and benefits of concessions.

In addition, by universally extending the benefits of liberalization to both liberal and protectionist nations, and to those more as well as to those less inclined to abide by agreeed-upon trading rules, national treatment and unconditional MFN would reduce the expected value of agreement for politically powerful nations, airlines, and labor interests. Strengthened provisions for remedies and dispute settlement can mitigate, but cannot solve, the underlying problem.

Finally, the application of national treatment and unconditional MFN is likely to discriminate against the more liberal nations' carriers. Since air services appear to be characterized by substantial economies of scope that can be realized only by operating an extensive route network, unconditional MFN and national treatment would afford important advantages to nations whose airlines enjoyed wide access to the markets of competitors while denying those competitors comparable access to their own markets.

To avoid the problems associated with unconditional MFN, negotiators could develop instead a conditional MFN agreement that would extend benefits only to those nations prepared to abide by its terms. A similar approach, modified to encompass the problem of market equivalence, might be applied to the national treatment principle as well (see Chapter 7).

Take Steps to Reduce the Risks of Liberalization

The GATT can also be a useful source for approaches that encourage liberal agreements by reducing the risks to the parties of making liberalizing concessions. The device of tariff bindings, for example, could prove particularly useful.[6] Bindings might best be described as doubly contingent promises. Like the exchange of promises that constitute a contract, bindings are made in exchange for the promises of others (that is, concessions). Unlike a contract at common law, however, a binding may be withdrawn without putting a party in breach of the agreement. Rather, the other parties have the right to withdraw promises (concessions) made in exchange for the withdrawn binding. Damagcs are thus limited to the withdrawal of concessions made in reliance on the retracted commitment.

Bindings can facilitate agreement by giving parties a legal avenue to withdraw concessions, thereby reducing the risks involved in experimenting with expanded trade liberalization. At the same time, the right of the other parties to withdraw comparable concessions serves as both a deterrent to withdrawal and an assured, prompt remedy—somewhat akin to liquidated damages.

U.S. air service negotiators have explicitly introduced the concept of bindings in at least one set of bilateral air service negotiations. During negotiations with Japan in the early 1980s, the U.S. delegation proposed bindings to deal with the difficult issue of airport access. Under that proposal, both the United States and Japan would grant expanded access to the carriers of the other party. If a party subsequently restricted that access (due, for example, to airport capacity or environmental reasons), the other party would be entitled to equivalent access at alternative airports or, at its option, to reduce the access granted to the airlines of the first party.[7] While not specifically called bindings, the United States has used similar techniques in order to deal with specific air services problems, including pricing[8] and routing.[9]

Although some might object to the uncertain commitments resulting from bindings, air services currently operate under bilateral agreements that permit complete termination upon one year's notice. Thus, actual practice suggests that nations and airlines are not deterred from agreement by the prospect that it may be terminated on short notice. Furthermore, by reducing the risks of liberalization to the contracting parties, bindings and similar devices add a measure of flexibility that apparently facilitates agreement. Similarly, the GATT experience with the use of tariff bindings seemingly has not discouraged tariff reductions. Bindings could also be used as one type of commitment within a larger agreement. Some parts of the agreement might be full contractual obligations, for example, while other portions could be made up of bindings.

SUMMARY

U.S. airline deregulation has demonstrated the competitive importance of establishing an extensive network of interconnected hubs, each with multiple spokes, in order to gain the significant economies of scope available to large airlines. The key to capturing these economies lies in the development of a viable hub operation that permits an airline to combine small traffic flows from a large number of points, thereby supporting a larger number of flights than would otherwise be economically feasible.

Although some GATT principles and procedures could be used for air services, the application of unconditional MFN and national treatment would give airlines from protectionist nations a distinct advantage by permitting them to develop more comprehensive networks than airlines from liberal countries. In addition, existing GATT dispute-resolution procedures may be too slow to deprive the breaching party of the benefits of its breach. Unless processes can be developed to provide prompt and flexible remedies, many nations, including the United States, will be less willing to negotiate significant new concessions.

Other features of the GATT approach, however, could contribute to air service liberalization. The concept of tariff bindings, for example, could be adapted to encourage greater willingness to risk trade liberalizing concessions. National treatment applied to areas other than such major economic rights as routes could also lead to important liberalizations in the air services. Even the MFN concept—transformed from unconditional to conditional MFN—may hold the key to a widespread liberalization of air services. Chapter 7, examines several possible strategies for liberalizing trade in air services.

NOTES

1. OECD Trade Committee, "Elements of a Conceptual Framework for Trade in Services," TC(87)2, January 1987.
2. Office of U.S. Trade Representative, "Services and the New Round," undated document.

3. Kenneth Dam, "Intellectual Property," *The International Lawyer* (Summer 1987).
4. "Groping for a New Order on Trade," *New York Times*, 30 August 1987.
5. "Groping for a New Order on Trade."
6. General Agreement on Tariffs and Trade, Article 2.
7. U.S.-Japan Air Services Negotiations, 1980–1983, from author's notes. Japanese air transport negotiators ultimately rejected this approach, and the problem of restrictions on airport access has yet to be resolved.
8. 1978 Exchange of Letters on Low Fares, Air Services Agreement Between the Government of the United States of America and the Government of the United Kingdom and Northern Ireland.
9. U.S.-Swiss Memorandum of Understanding signed in Davos, 1985.

7

NEGOTIATING CONSIDERATIONS

For the first time since the creation of the GATT over forty years ago, the success of major trade negotiations may well hinge on the ability of negotiators and governments to reexamine fundamental assumptions about the structure and process of trade negotiations, to abandon some basic tenets of the GATT approach, and to develop different, more flexible approaches to trade liberalization in service sectors.

The U.S. liberalization initiative in air services has demonstrated that it is possible for a few key bilaterals to break down protectionistic barriers and substantially increase competition (and consumer welfare), even for travel to protectionist countries. By using the "carrot" of access to a large traffic base and the "stick" of traffic diversion through adjacent liberal gateways, the United States has substantially deregulated air services between the United States and Europe. Likewise, strong U.S. pressure has led to some liberalization with Japan and significant liberalization with other Pacific rim countries. In addition, the U.S. effort has spawned movement toward deregulation in airline markets around the globe.

Nonetheless, further efforts to negotiate liberalized trade in air services, whether bilateral or multilateral, must be able to satisfy consumers, airlines, labor, and governments, all of whom ask What's in it for us? This will not be an easy task for a mature industry accustomed to receiving substantial protection from the rigors of competition. Nor will it be easy to convince privately owned airlines that a GATT-type regime can ensure fair competition with foreign airlines that are extensions of their national governments. Finally, neither governments accustomed to exerting significant control over their nations' airlines nor a labor force shielded by airline regulation can be expected to embrace liberalizing changes that weaken their present positions.

In terms of air services, the United States starts the Uruguay Round from a somewhat more advantageous position than that of other nations. With a large deregulated domestic market and liberal international agreements (including valuable intra-Asian and intra-European traffic rights), the U.S. airlines now enjoy a comfortable position in world aviation protected from foreign competition in a home market that, while highly competitive, is also large enough to generate substantial economies of scale and scope for both domestic and international operations.

But America faces a dilemma in considering further liberalization. As a large and efficient provider of air services, it could gain substantially by an opening access to worldwide markets. Yet the rest of the world appears to lack institutional capability of negotiating major liberalization of air services markets. Since the gains available from a bilateral liberalization of air services are largely exhausted, future gains are more likely to arise from multilateral agreements. For these, the GATT is a logical vehicle.

WHERE DO WE GO FROM HERE?

Bilateral Initiatives

Bilateral efforts to liberalize trade in air services are attractive in a number of ways. Bilaterals are a universally accepted method of negotiating air services agreements. By limiting the benefits of agreement to specific partners, bilaterals permit negotiators to experiment with liberalization on a limited basis. Equally important, bilaterals permit a nation to develop a package of economic rights to circumvent trade barriers that impede its airlines' competition in foreign markets.

Unfortunately, however, the bilateral system restrains as well as protects. After almost a decade of efforts to liberalize international air services through bilaterals, the United States appears to have realized most of the potential gains. U.S. airlines, regarded as among the world's most efficient and competitive, now find themselves unable to exercise their comparative advantage in other air service markets. Without the ability to offer access to a market as attractive as that of the United States, it is unlikely that other nations will be able to match U.S. gains under a bilateral regime.

An Umbrella Agreement

Another approach toward generic issues that affect air and other services would be to negotiate a GATT code defining a set of rules or understandings to apply across all (or most) service industries. Proponents of the so-called umbrella approach point out that it follows a well-established course in GATT negotiations. Furthermore, they note that developing such an agreement would be an efficient use of negotiating resources since it would establish a single set of rules and procedures for identifying and reducing barriers to expanded trade in all service sectors.

Nonetheless, multisectoral service negotiations would be plagued with major conceptual and practical problems. Even proponents of umbrella talks concede that progress would be slow, impeding liberalization in some sectors by lack of agreement in the more restrictive sectors. If air and financial services are primed for rapid liberalization, however, should progress in those sectors be restrained by difficulties in more problematic sectors such as shipping?

Even if the umbrella agreement provided only for minimum standards of liberalization that could be exceeded in individual sector negotiations, it is questionable whether the average degree of liberalization achieved would be greater than if the sectors pursued liberalization in a loosely coordinated set of sectoral negotiations without an umbrella agreement.

Furthermore, since any agreement that addressed the applicability of national treatment and MFN to air services would effectively determine a significant part of the package of substantive concessions, inclusion of those principles in the umbrella agreement would require umbrella negotiators to deal extensively with air services issues. Given the already formidable obstacles to reaching a liberalized services agreement, the negotiating process could be overwhelmed if it were burdened by the automatic extension of new rights inherent in national treatment and MFN. At a minimum, this approach would add complexity to a difficult undertaking. It would also tend to focus negotiations on limiting the applicability of the MFN and national treatment principles rather than on the more critical task of expanding effective market access for airlines. Neither outcome would advance the prospects for liberalization in air services nor, in all likelihood, for services overall.

An umbrella approach could also lead to intra-government conflicts between trade and sectoral officials. A proposal to shift services negotiating responsibility to the United States Trade Representative (USTR) would certainly provoke opposition by many affected industries and by the agencies that currently handle sectoral trade negotiations. Further, the USTR would be unable to master quickly the intricacies of several major new industries and would be dependent on the sector-specific agencies for expertise in any event.

Rather than alienating these essential sources of support and expertise, a more fruitful approach could be one that formed a U.S. government umbrella group, probably at the Cabinet Council level and chaired by a Cabinet officer with major economic and trade policy responsibility. This group would develop coordinated U.S. negotiating strategies, tactics, and positions for the service negotiations, which could be conducted on a bilateral, regional, or global basis and could cover single or multiple sectors.

This approach might be accurately described as a "common law" approach in which decentralized negotiations are controlled and coordinated by "a constitution" and by "judicial review," both emanating from the U.S. government's coordinating umbrella group. In contrast, the GATT-style multilateral umbrella agreement is comparable to a "code-based" legal system in which a detailed charter is agreed upon and thereafter negotiating solutions are derived by applying the code's provisions to specific situations. Particularly for an economy, and a polity, as pluralistic as that of the United States, the advantages of a common law approach to such complex trade negotiations should not be dismissed lightly.

Such an approach would neither preclude nor depend upon successfully negotiating a services umbrella agreement. So long as U.S. negotiators coordinate their positions, lack of progress on an umbrella agreement need not impair liberalization efforts in other sectors such as air services.

In addition to making virtue out of necessity, organizing ourselves before we try to organize the rest of the world would encourage a consistent U.S. approach toward principles and policies. It would also retain the advantages of flexibility and creativity inherent in decentralized organizations while providing a new and useful vehicle for U.S. negotiators to share ideas and to learn from the experiences of other U.S. negotiators. Finally, starting with the U.S. government instead of first seeking a multilateral umbrella agreement could easily result in better, timelier agreements.

A Targeted Multilateral Agreement

Since agreement among relatively few countries would cover well over one-half of all civil air traffic, a "super-GATT" for air services based on conditional MFN would be both easier to negotiate and considerably more liberal than any agreement based on the application of the principles of unconditional MFN and national treatment. Under these circumstances, a better approach would be to seek agreement among a relatively small group of liberal trading partners, initially involving the major air service powers and others willing to be bound by a more liberal regime. The targeted approach could mitigate the inherent lowest-common-denominator problem that plagues the GATT and simplify negotiations by limiting initial participation to those nations that shared broadly consistent interests.

Focusing on a relatively small group of nations with open, market-based economies and unsubsidized (and perhaps privately owned) airlines would allow negotiators to reach agreement more readily on the requisites for a truly liberal and competitive air services regime. Other nations wishing to participate in the expanded market access made available under this agreement would have to satisfy highest-common-denominator entry standards—elimination of subsidies and privatization of a national flag airline, changes in domestic regulatory policies, elimination of local computer reservation system monopolies, and acceptance of binding dispute resolution procedures.

The targeted approach would also strengthen negotiators from "rules-oriented" economies domestically by allowing them to link market-access concessions to enforceable reductions in other barriers impeding their national airlines' access to international traffic.

An agreement between the United States and Europe is the logical starting point for developing a targeted multilateral air services agreement. Both have large, well-developed internal air service markets served by established airlines, and the impending 1992 target for an internal EC market in air services is likely to strengthen the internal market and the surviving European airlines. In addition, well-established vehicles for discussions between European governments (under the auspices of the European Civil Aviation Conference and the European Community) and the United States provide a ready institutional framework for negotiating a targeted multilateral.

The Wait-and-See Approach. It is thus becoming increasingly clear on both sides of the Atlantic that the critical question is not whether the United States and Europe will negotiate a multilateral air services agreement, but rather when and how. At present, Washington and much of Europe appear content to wait for the EC to establish an internal common market in air services before beginning major U.S.-Europe negotiations. In light of the difficulties of forging an internal consensus on air services among Community members, the protectionist sentiments in Congress, and the lack of strong interest by U.S. airlines, it is not surprising that the lame duck Reagan administration might favor a strategy of wait and see.

By failing to press aggressively for liberalization, however, the United States may miss, perhaps irretrievably, a significant opportunity to help shape a more open, competitive worldwide market for air services. A decision to wait for Europe to formulate a common market is risky for several reasons.

First, by lessening the economic pressure on Europe to move rapidly toward liberalization, a wait-and-see approach strengthens those in Europe opposed to a more open, competitive air services regime. Without the threat of an active U.S. effort to liberalize air services further (and divert traffic from the airlines of illiberal nations), the process of liberalization will be slowed not only across the North Atlantic but within the European Community as well.

Second, such a decision is almost certain to delay U.S.-European liberalization far past 1992 and may diminish European nations' willingness to pursue broader liberalization in the air services. It is simply not realistic to expect Europe to engage in substantial market-opening negotiations with the United States on the heels of bruising internal EC negotiations. And even if the governments were willing to talk, they would find it extremely difficult to rally domestic support for trades with the United States that effectively unraveled the (no doubt) delicate compromises made during the internal EC negotiations. Thus, by waiting for Europe, the United States, the Community, and the world could be faced with another odious C.A.P.—this time, a Common Aviation Policy—by 1995.

Third, as the prime mover behind airline deregulation and in the broader effort to liberalize trade in services, the United States should have a strong policy interest in advancing liberalization in the highly visible airline industry. Further, the United States is institutionally and ideologically more committed to a market-based system than are many other nations, and its failure to take the lead would weaken the cause of liberalization.

Finally, changes in the world airline industry may well force governments to accept multilateralism long before the deadline for establishing an internal European common market. Multinational airline consortia that provide computerized reservations systems are currently in place, and transnational affiliations are not far behind. SAS and Sabena have publicly acknowledged negotiations aimed at integrating their airline operations, and the chairman of Alitalia has announced that he is seeking a merger partner. Indeed, airline executives, particularly in Europe, view an era of the "global airline" as inevitable. Unless governments act quickly to establish a liberal international regime, the emergence of multinational global airlines may force the establishment of a new regime.

A Plurilateral Initiative. If waiting for Europe is risky, what, then, can be done to advance liberalization in the air services sector? The most dramatic and effective step would be for the United States to invite several of its key aviation trading partners (Britain, the Netherlands, Belgium, Canada, and the Scandinavian countries) to negotiate a liberalized agreement among themselves.

This small group of nations with competitive airlines and market-oriented economies could establish a truly liberal regime. To obtain the benefits of expanded access to the internal and international markets of these initial signatories, subsequent signatories would have to meet the same high standards applied to the original signatories. Such an agreement would strengthen the pressure for liberalization both by setting high standards for the broader services negotiations and by reducing the ability of protectionist governments to dilute liberalizing measures to the lowest common denominator.

The point is not that negotiations among a small group of liberal countries would be easy—only that such negotiations would be less complex than those among a larger, more diverse group of nations. Even among relatively like-minded countries, governments will be required to make difficult changes in long-standing policies. Governments will have to reduce or eliminate their subsidies (and possibly ownership) of airlines, give foreign carriers broad access to domestic and inter-regional markets, and permit the acquisition of existing airlines and the establishment of new ones in their markets. They will also have to accept the inevitability of acquisitions, mergers, and the multinationalization of airlines formerly viewed as national flag carriers.

The negotiations will need to provide an equitable adjustment mechanism for the accession of new signatories. The United States, for example, is unlikely to accord British carriers full access to the domestic U.S. market until it is assured that American carriers will have access in Europe via Britain comparable to that of British carriers. Since Britain alone cannot ensure such access—the consent of other European states is also required—British rights in an initial agreement would presumably reflect the limited rights (between Britain, the Netherlands, and Scandinavia, for instance) assured to the United States. The prospect of additional signatories, however, would require some mechanism for increasing signatories' rights to reflect the increased value of the expanded agreement to the United States.

The economic pressures that now make air services ripe for liberalization will not await the outcome of marathon negotiations. If governments cannot act quickly enough to change the existing regime, these forces will find the "fault lines" in the existing system and force a restructuring of the world airline industry along the path of least resistance. Such a restructuring is likely to be neither as efficient nor as liberal as a regime negotiated among liberal trading partners.

The key to building a more liberal regime for air services is to capitalize on the pressure created by deregulation to create a market-based regime in air services. As the world's leading civil aviation power and its largest air services market, the United States is the logical, if not the only, candidate for the leading role in that effort. It remains to be seen whether America is prepared to respond to the casting call.

Index

ABOUT THE AUTHOR

Daniel M. Kasper is the director of transportation practice for Harbridge House, an international management consulting firm. Previously he served at the Civil Aeronautics Board, as executive assistant to the vice chairman of the Board and director of the Board's Bureau of International Aviation, where his responsibilities included international negotiations, route awards, and pricing. Mr. Kasper represented the Board before Cabinet and sub-Cabinet level officials from the Department of State, Transportation, and Justice, as well as before the Council of Economic Advisors. He also represented the Board at major international negotiations, including those between the United States and twenty-two West European countries that produced the first multilateral agreement deregulating international aviation pricing. Prior to joining the Civil Aeronautics Board, Mr. Kasper was a member of the faculty of the Harvard University Graduate School of Business Administration. He also taught at the University of Southern California Graduate School of Business Administration. He has written a number of case studies, research papers, and articles on the transportation industry, including *U.S. Regional Airlines Industry to 1996: Marketing Competition and the Demand for Aircraft*. Mr. Kasper received M.B.A. and J.D. degrees from the University of Chicago and holds an A.B. degree from Kansas University.